THE NIVELLE
AND T
BATTLE OF THE AISNE
1917

Craonnelle, photographed during the war from the local château (Stop 15).

THE NIVELLE OFFENSIVE AND THE BATTLE OF THE AISNE 1917

A Battlefield Guide to the Chemin des Dames

Andrew Uffindell

Pen & Sword
MILITARY

First published in Great Britain in 2015 by
PEN & SWORD MILITARY
an imprint of
Pen & Sword Books Ltd
47 Church Street
Barnsley
South Yorkshire
S70 2AS

ISBN 978 1 78303 034 7

A CIP catalogue record for this book is
available from the British Library.

Typeset in Palatino and Optima by
CHIC GRAPHICS

Printed and bound in England
by CPI Group (UK) Ltd, Croydon, CR0 4YY

Pen & Sword Books Ltd incorporates the imprints of
Pen & Sword Archaeology, Atlas, Aviation, Battleground, Discovery,
Family History, History, Maritime, Military, Naval, Politics, Railways,
Select, Social History, Transport, True Crime, Claymore Press,
Frontline Books, Leo Cooper, Praetorian Press, Remember When,
Seaforth Publishing and Wharncliffe.

For a complete list of Pen & Sword titles please contact
PEN & SWORD BOOKS LTD
47 Church Street, Barnsley, South Yorkshire, S70 2AS, England
E-mail: enquiries@pen-and-sword.co.uk
Website: www.pen-and-sword.co.uk

CONTENTS

ACKNOWLEDGEMENTS

I am much indebted to Rupert Harding and the team at Pen & Sword Books for their helpfulness throughout this project. I am also very grateful to my family and friends for their support and encouragement, and to my editor, Sarah Cook. I wish to thank the staff at numerous museums and libraries, including the *Bayerische Staatsbibliothek* at Munich, the *Archives départementales de l'Aisne* at Laon, the *Service historique de la défense* at Vincennes, the *Bibliothèque de documentation internationale contemporaine* at Nanterre, the British Library and the Imperial War Museum at London, the National Archives at Kew, and Hertfordshire county library services. Thank you also to Gilles Chauwin and the inhabitants of the Chemin des Dames region.

The whitish layer in this trench is the stone roadway of the Chemin des Dames. The earth on top was excavated when the trench was dug.

Trench mortars: the Monument des crapouillots (Tour III).

KEY TO MAPS

Unit symbols:

□	British
▨	French
■	German
⊠	Infantry
⬭	Armour
XXXXX	Army group
XXXX	Army
XXX	Corps (or Gruppe)
XX	Division
X	Brigade (or infantry groupement)
III	Regiment
II	Battalion (or armoured groupement)
I	Company (or armoured groupe)
---xx---	Boundary between French divisions

Examples:

3 ⊠ 152 (with II above)	3rd Battalion of French 152e régiment d'infanterie
1 ⬭ (with I above)	AS1 (French armoured groupe)
bR 5 ⊠ (with xx above)	Bavarian 5. Reserve-Infanterie-Division

The unit's designation is shown by the letters or numbers on the left of the symbol. The number on the right is that of the parent regiment.

Other symbols:

⤬	*British / Commonwealth*
◫	*French*
▬	*German*
▤	*US*
⌇◫	*French front line*
⌇⬤	*German trench*
★	*Fort*
☆	*Cavern*
◉	*Church*
⊞	*Cemetery*
△	*Monument*
P	*Parking*
M	*Museum*
✳	*Viewpoint*
⠿	*Wood or forest (or remnants after shelling)*
⬯	*Pond or lake*
∿	*River*
··········	*Canal*
▬▪▬	*Railway*
▬▬▬	*Motorway or dual carriageway*
═══	*Road*
-------	*Footpath, track or minor road unsuitable for vehicles*

Altitudes are in metres.

Abbreviations:

AS:	Artillerie spéciale, or artillerie d'assaut (tanks)
b:	bayerisch (Bavarian)
BCP:	Bataillon de chasseurs à pied
BEF:	British Expeditionary Force
CAC:	Corps d'armée colonial
DI:	Division d'infanterie
DIC:	Division d'infanterie coloniale
Dmt spéc:	Détachement spécial
Gd:	Garde (Guard)
GdGr:	Garde-Grenadier
LNL:	Loyal North Lancashire Regiment
Lw:	Landwehr
R:	Reserve
RI:	Régiment d'infanterie
RIA:	Régiment d'infanterie alpine
RIC:	Régiment d'infanterie coloniale
RICM:	Régiment d'infanterie coloniale du Maroc
T:	Tirailleurs
Z:	Zouaves
ZT:	(Régiment mixte de) zouaves et de tirailleurs

INTRODUCTION

Even today, the Chemin des Dames remains bitterly controversial. No other great French battle of the First World War provokes such overwhelmingly negative and uncomfortable reactions. The Marne in 1914 is remembered as a miraculous salvation, and the defence of Verdun two years later as an intensely symbolic triumph, yet the Chemin des Dames remains entrenched in popular memory as a byword for futile bloodbaths and is for ever linked to the notorious crisis of discipline that paralysed the French army in the middle of 1917.

The defining feature of the battlefield is a road hugging the crest of a long, jagged plateau north of the Aisne river with spectacular views over the surrounding countryside. The route is an ancient one, and according to popular legend was paved in the 1780s to make it easier for the daughters of King Louis XV – the *Mesdames de France* – to visit one of their ladies-in-waiting. The road hence became known as the Chemin des Dames, and its name is also applied by extension to the plateau.

Almost the entire area of the Chemin des Dames has been cleared of debris and returned to use, making it hard to imagine the desolation that blighted it at the war's end. 'Coarse grass has grown up already on some parts of the battlefield', noted the writer Violet Markham in the spring of 1919, 'but in the main the surface is a series of shell holes filled with stagnant water, green [and] disgusting.' What struck her most during this visit was the deep and unsettling silence: 'It is the outstanding feature of the devastated areas, that and the disappearance of all human life. So great is the sense of oppression, one ends by speaking almost in half-tones.'

Venturing into this empty landscape in the early 1920s made the novelist Roman Dorgelès feel like someone exploring a newly discovered continent:

What semblance of civilisation remains on these chalky slopes? Not a road, not a tree, not a shack. This outline of a path –

A group of US ladies visiting the Chemin des Dames, c.1919.

recognisable despite its ravaged state and the craters left by the shelling – is the Chemin des Dames. For fifty months men fought for it, slitting each other's throats while the world waited on tenterhooks to find out whether the little path had finally been gained. Yet that famous Chemin was no more than this: with a single stride you've left it behind . . .

Just 100 km to the south-west of this wasteland lay the great city of Paris. It was the proximity of Paris that made the Chemin des Dames so important. The plateau was a natural bulwark blocking the most direct invasion route into the heart of France from the Belgian frontier. Sandwiched between the Aisne and Ailette rivers, it was an obvious position on which to check an advance heading either north or south.

A modern-day kilometre-marker on the Chemin des Dames. The 'D' signifies a secondary road maintained by the local département. The 'CD' is a reminder of its historic name.

In September 1914, it was on the Chemin des Dames that the Western Front stabilized in the wake of the German retreat from the Battle of the Marne. British and French attempts to conquer the crucial plateau were narrowly foiled as the Germans rushed reinforcements to the scene. In October, the French took over the entire sector, so the British Expeditionary Force could leave the Aisne in order to move north and cover the Channel ports. Fighting on the Chemin des Dames died down towards the end of November as attention shifted elsewhere. It flared up again briefly in January 1915, but otherwise the area ceased to be a point of friction for well over two years.

In fact, the Chemin des Dames remained a quiet sector for most of the war. The three great Battles of the Aisne in September 1914, mid-1917 and May 1918 inevitably command attention, but they were exceptional. Units were brought here to rest, and the German *7. Armee*, which held this part of the front, was dubbed the *schlafende Heer,* or 'sleeping army'. Not until the first months of 1917, as evidence grew of an impending French attack, did this sleepiness give way to feverish activity.

1917: year of crisis
Britain and France had no option but to take the offensive in 1917. It was vital for them to retain the initiative and exploit the damage done to the German army by the Battle of the Somme. They were also under pressure to end the war victoriously while they still had a significant advantage of numbers on the Western Front and before the erosion of domestic support forced them to seek a compromise peace.

Both sides had spent the past two years mobilizing ever greater resources. As exhaustion set in, they now faced the prospect of a decline in their armies' manpower and a series of political, social and economic crises. All the belligerents would be affected by these strains to a greater or lesser extent during 1917. In France, the national unity forged at the start of the war was breaking down. Weariness made the country impatient, and in December 1916 months of friction between the high command and an increasingly assertive parliament culminated in the removal of the generalissimo, *Général de division* Joseph Joffre. The man who replaced him as commander-in-chief of the French armies on the Western Front was the 60-year-old *Général de division* Robert Nivelle, a charismatic and politically acceptable figure who had enjoyed a meteoric rise since 1914 – from *colonel* commanding an artillery regiment to commander-in-chief in just twenty-six months.

Nivelle.

Nivelle's successful attacks at Verdun in October and December 1916 convinced him that he had discovered the formula for victory, based on a massive use of artillery firepower. He wanted to replicate those methods on a larger scale, and amended the plans that Joffre had made for a general offensive in February 1917. Not content with methodically grinding down the crust of the German front with a series of blows, Nivelle sought to smash right through it within forty-eight hours and precipitate a decisive battle of manoeuvre in the open country. His approach was an extreme solution, in tune with the prevailing frustration at the deadlock. The other key change Nivelle made was to switch the main effort to the Aisne, so he could thrust northwards into the flank of the great German salient that bulged westwards between Soissons and Arras. (Joffre had planned to hammer away in the area of the Somme, with just a secondary attack on the Aisne, but Nivelle thought the Somme unlikely to produce rapid results since the region was so devastated and strongly held.)

Fatal delays

A series of delays pushed back the start of Nivelle's offensive until April. The underlying problem was the difficulty in coordinating an array of Allied onslaughts on multiple fronts so as to exert the greatest possible pressure on the Central Powers. Both the Russians and the Italians were becoming a spent force, and neither of them proved able to support Nivelle with simultaneous offensives of their own.

While the Allies were in disarray, a new German command team was taking a series of key decisions. In August 1916, *Generalfeldmarschall* Paul von Hindenburg was appointed Chief of the General Staff, with *General der Infanterie* Erich Ludendorff as his deputy. Numerical weakness forced them to remain on the defensive on the Western Front, but in the middle of March 1917 they abandoned the massive, exposed salient between Arras and Soissons and fell back to a newly prepared position, the so-called *Siegfried-Stellung*. Besides disrupting Allied plans, the withdrawal shortened the line by 40 km and helped build up the German reserves on the Western Front to an unprecedented size.

A new tactical doctrine also emerged. It was a mistake, the Germans realized, to hold their first line rigidly with large numbers of troops. Instead, they were moving towards the concept of a more flexible defence-in-depth. By creating zones 8 to 12 km deep, consisting of a succession of positions with concealed machine-gun nests scattered across the intervening terrain, they made it difficult for an attacker to break through in a single blow. The foremost position consisted of three trench-lines and was known as the *I Stellung*. Some 2 or 3 km behind it lay an intermediate position, the *Artillerie-Schutzstellung*, which protected the battery emplacements. Even further back was a *II Stellung*, possibly supported by a third.

By reducing the numbers of troops in the front line, the Germans were able to keep powerful reserves in hand. Specially trained *Eingreif-Divisionen*, or intervention divisions, stood near the back of the defensive zone to counter any break-in. An enemy attack could thus be met by a series of prompt, vigorous and progressively stronger counter-thrusts before it had time to consolidate its gains. These counter-thrusts sought not to recapture every piece of ground regardless of cost, but rather to establish a strong and cohesive position in which to continue the battle.

This defensive doctrine evolved during 1917, and was adapted as the Allies changed their methods of attack. It was refined above all in Flanders, in the face of powerful and persistent British attacks. Only a limited version was applied on the Chemin des Dames, partly because of the nature of the terrain – in many places the plateau was too steep and narrow for a deep defence – and partly because of concern in some quarters about the risks of relying too heavily on the intervention of the *Eingreif-Divisionen*, which required perfect timing.

Riddled with doubts

On 4 April, Nivelle amended his plan to take account of the German withdrawal to the *Siegfried-Stellung*. Some of his intended secondary attacks were no longer possible or had to be reduced in scale. The main attack on the Aisne became even more important, and Nivelle added a

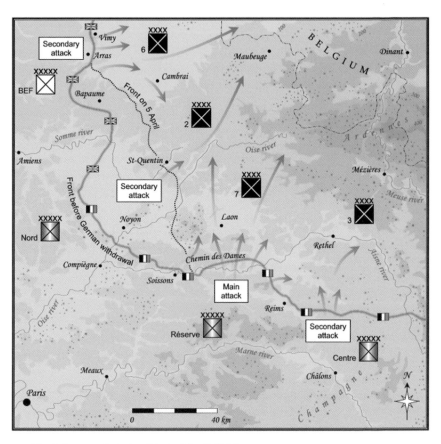

Nivelle's amended plan (start of April 1917).

new secondary attack east of Reims. The finalized plan was for a series of onslaughts, staggered in time so they began in the north and gradually spread along the Western Front over the course of a week. The first attacks – by the British near Arras and the *Groupe d'armées du Nord* at Saint-Quentin – were intended to pin down German reserves in the north. The *Groupe d'armées de réserve* would then launch the main attack in the Chemin des Dames sector. It would be seconded a day later by an attack east of Reims by the *Groupe d'armées du Centre*.

Yet two pivotal events had transformed the strategic situation in just three weeks. Revolution in Russia forced Tsar Nicholas II to abdicate on 15 March, and on 6 April the United States declared war on Germany. Combined with the German withdrawal to the *Siegfried-Stellung*, these two developments called into question the whole basis on which Nivelle's plans had been made, as they rendered Russian support uncertain but offered the long-term prospect of US reinforcements offsetting France's own declining manpower.

The French government was right to consider whether the impending offensive should still be mounted on so ambitious a scale, but it did so in a confused and indecisive way during an informal council-of-war with Nivelle and his three army group commanders at Compiègne on 6 April. The idea of cancelling the offensive was dismissed, but the government failed to take a clear-cut decision as to whether to restrict it to more modest objectives. This was yet another symptom of the political weakness and instability that dogged France throughout most of 1917. Alexandre Ribot's ministry was just two-and-a-half weeks old. It desired a prompt end to the war, yet was nervous about the prospect of heavy casualties and could not decide whether or not it retained confidence in the commander-in-chief. When Nivelle tendered his resignation, it was refused, yet the doubts voiced by both politicians and some of his subordinates had undermined his authority before the offensive had even begun.

Chemin des Dames
Nivelle has been harshly criticized for attacking the Chemin des Dames. The plateau looms some 90 to 130 metres above the adjacent valleys of the Aisne and Ailette, and its steep sides form an intricate series of spurs jutting out from the long, central crest. The complexity of the terrain hardly favoured the rapid progress on which Nivelle counted. Even after conquering the plateau, his men would have to cross another 10–15 km of valleys and ridges until they reached the vast, open plain that surrounded the hilltop city of Laon.

But if not on the Chemin des Dames, where could Nivelle attack? Few alternative sectors were suitable, either because they were too distant from the secondary attacks in the north, or because they were pointed in the wrong direction or had already been devastated by earlier battles. Despite its formidable appearance, the Chemin des Dames was not impregnable, for ground is only as strong as the troops available to hold it and much depends on the circumstances under which it is attacked. Unfortunately for the French, they lacked the advantage of surprise, for the sheer scale of the offensive made the preparations obvious to German observers watching from the high ground or from the air, and there were some notorious security leaks. This made a thorough artillery preparation even more essential to success. Nivelle insisted that it should target the entire depth of the defensive zone, so the infantry could break right through without having to pause for batteries to be brought forward for a renewed bombardment directed against the rearmost positions. Yet in practice the artillerymen proved unable to devastate the whole zone beforehand, for only their most powerful guns could hit the furthest positions. Bad weather and German superiority in the air hindered observation, and difficulties with resupplying ammunition made it impossible to maintain the intensity of the preparation when it was extended by four days.

The *Groupe d'armées de réserve* had an attack front of 40 km. Soissons and Reims – key road and rail hubs – were in French hands and formed bastions on either flank. The greatest German vulnerability in this sector lay in the west, where they held a salient bulging 5 km in front of the crest of the Chemin des Dames as far as the Aisne river at

Nivelle offensive, 16 April 1917.

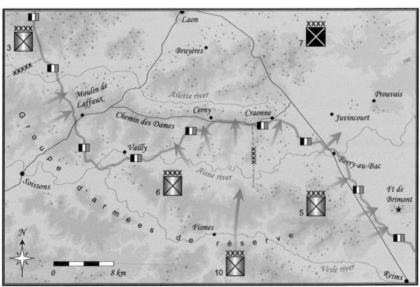

Prisoners: captured German soldiers pass along a communication trench on their way to the rear.

Vailly. The French intended to pinch out this salient by launching their attacks on either side of it. Two armies – the *6e* and *5e armées* – were to smash through the German defensive zone, and then a third, the *10e armée*, would be inserted in between them to exploit the success.

After several postponements, the attack was fixed for the morning of 16 April. One of the French infantrymen waiting in support was *Caporal* Georges Gaudy. 'The noise [of the artillery] fired us up,' he wrote. 'We felt tired no longer, and instead became impatient as we awaited the hour.' Looking behind him, he saw that the hills south of the Aisne were black with troops. 'Everywhere shone the blue helmets. Our enthusiasm grew, increasing tenfold at the thought that we had all these men massed behind, and these experienced soldiers in front of us.'

Yet the breakthrough never came. In most sectors, the gains on that first day were no more than 1 or 2 km deep. On the 17th, Nivelle altered the axis of the offensive so as to bypass the Chemin des Dames, in the hope of securing a breakthrough to the north-east instead of directly to the north. The main effort now fell to the *5e armée* in the plain below the eastern end of the plateau. The *6e armée* was simply to cover its left flank and make local attacks on the Chemin des Dames.

Nivelle did have one important success. On 18 April, the Germans abandoned their endangered salient at Vailly and pulled back to the crest of the Chemin des Dames. The front line of the *6e armée* now ran all along the plateau, weaving slightly north and south of the road. But the *5e armée* failed to make progress, with bad weather on the 17th and 18th delaying its planned north-eastward thrust.

The first phase of the battle was drawing to a close. It was impossible to maintain the scale and tempo of the offensive, and a lull set in as early as the 19th. On the 21st, the commander of the *Groupe d'armées de réserve* wrote and urged Nivelle to make limited, attritional attacks to improve the existing positions rather than pursue illusory hopes of a breakthrough. Since the heights on either flank of the *5e armée* were still in German hands, any thrust across the plain to the north-east would be self-defeating as it would simply carve out a dangerously exposed salient.

Nivelle heeded these arguments. On 22 April, he ordered a switch to partial attacks for limited objectives. The *6e armée* was simply to complete the conquest of the Chemin des Dames plateau, helped on its right flank by the newly inserted *10e armée*. The *5e* and *4e armées* were to make combined attacks on either side of Reims, in order to push the Germans further away from the city.

The Chemin des Dames, 5 May 1917.

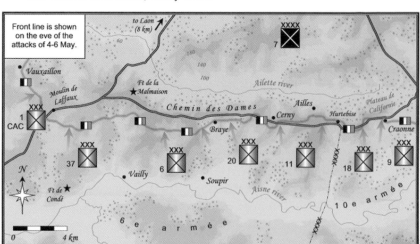

Chemin des Dames, 5 May 1917. French infantry surge forward.

Mounting these new attacks was delayed by bad weather, ammunition shortages, and the challenge of coordinating the plans of four armies in order to maximize their chances of success. Nivelle's indecisiveness worsened the problem, and political interference resulted in the *5e armée*'s attack being reduced in scale so as to limit the likely casualty figures. The attacks were eventually launched on 30 April (*4e armée*), 4 May (*5e armée*), and 5 May (*10e* and *6e armées*). Some tactical gains were made, but at a heavy cost. Both sides were exhausted.

The fallout
Nivelle's hopes of fighting a decisive campaign of manoeuvre had been progressively whittled down to a bludgeoning battle of attrition. Instead of smashing right through the German fortified zone at a stroke, he had merely broken into the foremost positions and saddled himself with a debilitating struggle. Yet his offensive was not a complete failure. The attacks immobilized and wore down the German reserves on the Western Front, and made significant local gains, though Nivelle might have achieved much of this at less cost by planning a series of less ambitious attacks from the start. The exact number of casualties will never be known, but the French official history estimated that the four armies in the Aisne–Champagne sector – the *4e, 5e, 6e* and *10e armées* –

lost up to 134,000 men killed, wounded or captured during the initial period between 16 and 25 April. Losses were not disproportionate in comparison with previous offensives, yet the result was perceived as a disaster because of the mismatch between the ambitious objectives and the actual results – a mismatch that was intolerable in the prevailing atmosphere of war-weariness and political impatience. Disappointment over the limited gains was aggravated by specific controversies, especially over the inadequate artillery preparation, the lack of surprise, the inability of the French aircraft to dominate the skies, and the fact that the medical service had been overwhelmed by the sheer numbers of casualties.

The government dithered over whether to sack Nivelle. Only on 15 May did it finally replace him with *Général de division* Philippe Pétain. Nivelle has been accused of over-confidence and a disregard for casualties, yet it was actually indecisiveness that characterized his period in command, and he found himself overwhelmed by a situation that was only partly of his making. He became a convenient scapegoat for wider failings, many of which were the government's responsibility. It was not just Nivelle's plan that failed in 1917, but the entire concept of colossal offensives that he had inherited. A switch to methods more in line with France's physical and moral strength was overdue.

The stark reality of the situation was underlined by the breakdown of discipline that now paralysed the French army. Disorders had started to break out on 29 April, and the scale of the crisis was unprecedented. Thousands of soldiers formed assemblies, demonstrated, threatened their officers, and refused to return to the front line. Many more men approved of what was happening without taking an active part. The disturbances have often been misinterpreted in the past – generals at the time were quick to blame subversion by pacifists and revolutionaries – and are still debated by historians today. They were sparked by a range of causes, and took a variety of forms, but only occasionally included violence. Most were short-lived and, although commonly known as mutinies, were more in the nature of military strikes. The German high command was at least partly aware of the crisis, but lacked the strength to mount a major offensive. In any case, the French continued to hold the front, for the soldiers objected not to defending their country but to mounting attacks whose losses seemed unjustified by the results.

Pétain's efforts to restore morale were well publicized. He is standing here in the centre, wearing a képi and grey moustache, while visiting the troops.

The disorders were most prevalent in the area behind the front that had been attacked in April–May, yet blaming them solely on Nivelle is over-simplistic. The frequency and seriousness of the incidents actually increased after 15 May – after the offensive had been suspended and after Nivelle had been replaced by Pétain. Not until the first week of June did the crisis reach its peak. The disturbances reflected the wider war-weariness in France. Tension had been building up for months, and it was the prevailing sense of drift and instability, worsened by strikes in France and revolution in Russia, that provided an opportunity for the crisis to break out. Nivelle's removal seems actually to have worsened the situation, since it reinforced the impression of disarray. It is also clear that Pétain played only a limited role in ending the crisis, adept though he was at portraying himself as a saviour. By the time his counter-measures could be implemented, the disorders were already subsiding – partly because units were correcting the backlog of overdue leave that had built up earlier.

Pétain's real importance was longer term. He began a thorough overhaul of the French army, including its tactics, training and equipment, and oversaw the completion of its transformation into a modern, industrialized military machine. Before attempting another general offensive he was determined to wait for an infusion of fresh US divisions and the production of an array of modern equipment – aircraft, artillery and tanks – in order to spare France's precious manpower and restore the army's shaken morale. His reforms fitted within the context of a remobilization of the French nation as a whole in pursuit of victory whatever the cost – a revival symbolized by the formation of a new, strong government in November under the formidable Georges Clémenceau.

Points of friction

Fighting on the Chemin des Dames continued throughout the summer. Neither side had enough resources to mount anything larger than local attacks, yet both had to continue attacking in order to improve their fragile positions. The Chemin des Dames could not become a quiet sector, held by reduced numbers of troops, so long as both opponents maintained a hold on the top of the plateau. At many points, the nature of the terrain made it difficult to give any depth to the defence, and so a rigid, forward defence was the only option, even though it wore out units more quickly. At stake was a string of observation points that dominated the Aisne or Ailette valleys, such as Le Panthéon, La Royère, Froidmont, the *Monument* at Hurtebise, and the sugar-beet refinery at Cerny, and their names became notorious.

Attrition ground down both sides. The purely local operations mounted by the French lacked sufficient power to prevent the Germans from making attacks of their own. Along the Chemin des Dames, frequent German onslaughts chipped away at the French gains and took a cumulatively heavy toll in lives. These carefully planned attacks were spearheaded by specially trained assault detachments, or *Stosstrupps*, and relied on a brief but violent bombardment to ensure surprise. It was imperative for the French to end this constant friction.

La Malmaison

Pétain had rejected any attempt to secure a breakthrough in the immediate future. He preferred to mount a series of more modest attacks on the Western Front with limited, achievable objectives. The great advantage of these 'bite-and-hold' attacks was that they could dismantle the German defensive system bit by bit, by securing a solid

Firepower: the 400mm railway howitzer was used by the French in the Malmaison offensive.

Loading a 400mm shell. These massive projectiles were particularly suitable for smashing creutes.

chunk of the foremost positions with the support of massive firepower, and then consolidating the gains in time to repel the inevitable counter-thrusts.

At the end of October, one of these operations seized the area of Fort de la Malmaison at the western end of the Chemin des Dames. The Malmaison offensive was the ultimate example of a set-piece attack mounted with overwhelming resources to achieve realistic objectives. The sheer power of the preliminary artillery bombardment practically guaranteed success. 'Compared to this drumfire, everything that had happened before was mere child's play,' wrote a German infantryman. 'There was no way we could stand in the open. If we had held out a finger, it was a dead certainty that it would have been shot off, such was the wildness in this hell that had been let loose.' The offensive forced the Germans to abandon the entire length of the Chemin des Dames, for their remaining positions on the plateau were now enfiladed by the French artillery.

Turning the tide

The Malmaison offensive brought closure at last to the relentless attrition on the Chemin des Dames. Yet the war as a whole was turning against the Allies. Russia's collapse and withdrawal from the conflict following the Bolshevik takeover in November shifted the balance of forces in the west, for not until the middle of the following year would trained US manpower become available in significant numbers.

In the spring of 1918, the Western Front was shaken by a series of German offensives, the third and most successful of which was unleashed on the Aisne on 27 May. The Allied forces holding the Chemin des Dames were overstretched and included four battered British divisions that had been sent to this supposedly quiet sector to rest. The local French army commander rejected the idea of an elastic defence-in-depth, partly as the Chemin des Dames had cost too much blood the previous year to be readily abandoned. Stunned by a hurricane bombardment, the Allied units were dislocated by the German infiltration tactics and paralysed by the superior tempo of the attack. As the defence fell apart, the onslaught flooded over the plateau and beyond the Aisne. Yet it eventually petered out, and the spectacular advance simply saddled the Germans with an unsustainable salient 35 km deep.

Within a couple of months the Allies had regained the initiative, and during the autumn they drove back the demoralized German army with offensives mounted in quick succession along the Western Front. A month before the armistice, the Chemin des Dames fell once more into Allied hands.

Nomenclature

Assigning different names and dates to an historical event can make subtle but significant differences to how it is perceived, and this is particularly true of the Nivelle offensive. The main onslaught within that offensive – the Second Battle of the Aisne – began on 16 April 1917, but both its duration and its geographical extent are open to interpretation. The closure date that has commonly been assigned to the battle is the middle of May, but this was politically convenient. Setting aside the subsequent success of the Malmaison offensive made it easier for Nivelle's detractors to criticize him for the disappointing results.

Separating the April–May attacks from those that followed is an artificial distinction, not least as the Malmaison offensive was mounted from ground conquered by Nivelle. 'The Battle of La Malmaison is not, in fact, a local operation isolated in time and space,' wrote a French army group commander, *Général de division* Louis Franchet d'Espèrey. 'On the contrary, it forms the decisive phase of the Battle of the Chemin des Dames that began on 16 April and ended on 2 November with the German withdrawal to the north of the Ailette.'

This guidebook covers the entire six-month period between April and October 1917. We shall focus on the Chemin des Dames, which is an area compact enough to be explored thoroughly within a week, but we must bear in mind that this was not an isolated battlefield. The so-called 'Nivelle offensive' actually involved a whole series of offensives along the Western Front, and the actions on the Chemin des Dames were linked particularly closely with those on the hills east of Reims – so closely that the Germans described them as a double-battle, the *Doppelschlacht Aisne-Champagne*.

ADVICE FOR TOURERS

Planning your visit

The Chemin des Dames lies within a triangle formed by the three cities of Laon, Soissons and Reims. They are ideal bases from which to explore the area, as the entire battlefield lies within a radius of under 50 km from any one of them. Reims is the largest, with a population of 180,000. Soissons has 29,000 inhabitants, and Laon 26,000.

Public transport services are limited outside these cities, so we advise you to travel around the region by car. The time required to visit the Chemin des Dames depends on how thoroughly you wish to explore it, but allow half-a-day for each of the five battlefield tours, and a week for a full and leisurely exploration of the entire area. Bear in mind that museums may be closed for part of the year, or plan major renovations to mark the centenary of the war. Contact details are given on page 188, to enable you to obtain up-to-date opening hours.

Safety precautions

The Chemin des Dames is sparsely populated, and few of the adjacent villages have shops or petrol stations. Details of local restaurants can be found in the tourist information sites listed on page 188. Take sensible precautions, and never touch unexploded ammunition or enter the numerous tunnels and quarries in the area. Be careful when walking along the Chemin des Dames: the road is not particularly busy, but the traffic is sometimes fast. Boots may prove useful on some of the tracks in wet weather.

How to use this book

The core of this guidebook consists of five tours examining key episodes of the battle. Although arranged in chronological order, they can be visited in any sequence. Each tour starts with an account of what happened and then explains what you can see on the ground today. Tour II is by far the longest at 35 km and should be driven. A car will be

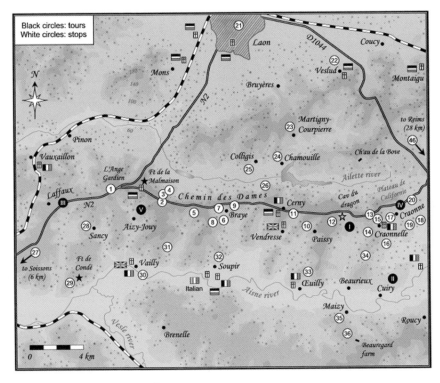

Touring the Chemin des Dames.

useful for most of Tours III and V, but some of their points of interest are inaccessible to vehicles. Tour IV is almost entirely a walking route, and Tour I is also best done on foot.

To supplement these tours, the 'Stops' section of this book covers forty-six specific locations on and near the Chemin des Dames. Choose which of these individual stops you wish to visit as you travel between the tours, depending on their proximity and the time you have available. The most worthwhile of them are the Caverne du dragon (Stop 12), Cerny (11), Fort de Condé (29), Soupir (32), Veslud (22), and the three cities of Soissons, Laon and Reims (27, 21 and 46).

Maps
To get the most out of your visit, you should obtain some road maps for use in conjunction with this book, along with a magnetic compass and

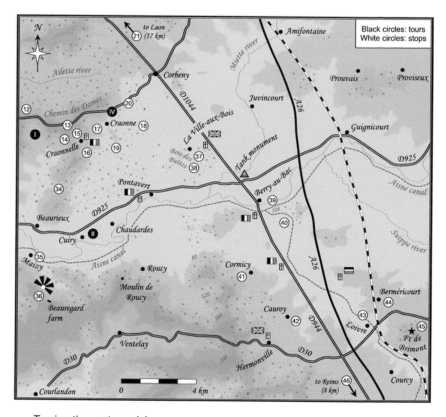

Touring the eastern plains.

a pair of binoculars. We recommend the *Top 100 Tourisme et découverte* series, published on a scale of 1:100,000 by the French *Institut géographique national (IGN)*. The following sheet covers the area of the Chemin des Dames:

104: Reims/Saint-Quentin

This map is adequate for navigating your way round the battlefield. But for exploring key sectors, you will benefit from the more detailed *IGN Série Bleu* maps, drawn on a scale of 1:25,000. The following are the relevant sheets:

2610 E: Anizy-le-Château
2710 O: Laon
2611 O: Soissons

2611 E: Braine [for Tours III and V]
2711 O: Beaurieux [for Tour I]
2711 E: Craonne [for Tour IV and most of Tour II]
2811 O: Guignicourt
2812 O: Reims

IGN maps can be obtained through the *Institut*'s website (www.ign.fr).

Historical notes

All times in this book have been standardized to French time. (In 1917 the Germans were normally one hour ahead, but French Summer Time came into effect during the night of 24/25 March and German Summer Time during the night of 15/16 April.)

In the French army, an *aspirant* was an officer designate, serving temporarily in an officer role while aspiring to be commissioned. A *caporal*, unlike a British corporal, was not an NCO rank.

Roads

Some roads have recently been reclassified, which may cause confusion if you are using older maps. In particular, the N44 linking Laon and Reims has been downgraded from a national to a *départemental* road. It is now the D1044 within the *département* of the Aisne, and the D944 within the Marne.

The N2 has been turned into a dual carriageway for almost the entire distance between Laon and Soissons. In some stretches, it now follows a slightly different route and bypasses various towns. As a result of these changes, the road junctions at l'Ange Gardien (Stop 1) and the moulin de Laffaux (Tour III) have been rearranged.

Monument des Basques (Stop 14).

TOURS

Tour I
Marchand's Division
16 April 1916

Our opening tour looks at the first day of the French offensive on the Aisne. We shall focus in detail on one of the most fascinating sectors, situated midway along the eastern half of the Chemin des Dames. Here, at Hurtebise farm, the plateau abruptly narrows to form a saddle of high ground just 130 metres broad. Nowhere else along its entire length does the summit of the Chemin des Dames shrivel into so tight a pinchpoint. The peculiar terrain both hindered and favoured the French attack – hindered it with the steepness and irregularity of the slopes that the infantry had to scale, but favoured it with the narrowness of the saddle, which made it difficult for the Germans to give any depth to their defence.

WHAT HAPPENED

Attacking this sector was the task of the easternmost formation of the *6e armée*, the crack *10e division d'infanterie coloniale*. Its commander was Jean-Baptiste Marchand, whose career had been blighted by the Fachoda Affair in 1898, when his expedition to the Upper Nile had ended with the French government backing down from a confrontation with the British. Intense, highly strung, and sometimes excessively brave, Marchand had already been wounded three times during the war. 'Pétain has spoken to him about his rashness,' wrote the commander of the *6e armée* in January 1917.

> I think that this was just a passing phase, and that he knows a divisional commander must stay in his command post during

an attack – indeed, he himself said as much very frankly. But ultimately, that is the least fault that should be criticized in this war, and we can not hold it against him for very long.

Marchand was so completely identified with his division, which he had led ever since its formation in May 1915, that it was known simply as the *Division Marchand*. At its core were three regiments of *infanterie coloniale*, the *33e, 52e* and *53e*. These élite French troops were nicknamed the *marsouins*, or 'porpoises' – a reminder that they had formerly been marines until their transfer to the army's control in 1900. Seven battalions of black soldiers, or *tirailleurs sénégalais*, had been added to strengthen the division, and three of these battalions were grouped together to form the *58e régiment*. The men came from French Black Africa as a whole, but were called Senegalese because the first of their battalions had been created in Senegal in 1857.

The division was organized into two infantry *groupements* deployed abreast. Within each *groupement*, the onslaught was spearheaded by a

Marchand's division, 16 April 1917.

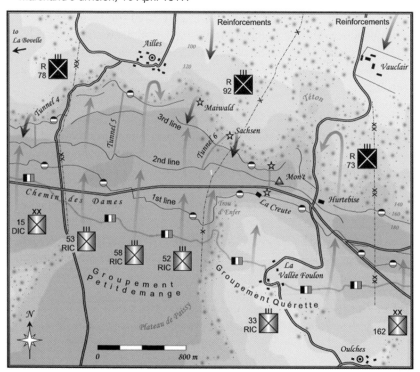

Senegalese battalion in the centre and a white one on either flank. The remaining battalions formed two successive echelons that were to pass through and take up the attack in turn once the units in front had gained specific objective lines. The first objective ran along the north bank of Ailette river, some 2.5 km away, and was to be reached in about an hour-and-a-half. Speed was essential. Each objective was to be taken in a single bound, by infantry advancing behind the protection of a rolling barrage and progressing at a rate of 100 metres every three minutes. As the plan of the army corps explained, it was vital to press on without being distracted by resistance on a flank:

> The assault waves will follow each other without pause, followed closely by the small reserve columns, so as to form an orderly, swift and coherent stream. Any remaining defensive systems of the enemy will be bypassed resolutely by the assault waves, and will find themselves swamped and at the mercy of the reserves. The enemy positions must therefore be attacked frontally, in a violent, brutal and swift action, in order to try to break through them. Positions that are especially strong or tenaciously defended must normally be made to fall by being bypassed as a result of the progression made in adjacent zones.

Formidable defences
The natural strength of the Chemin des Dames encouraged the Germans to try to hold the top of the plateau solidly. They intended to defeat the attack within a battlezone formed by the three successive trench-lines of the *I Stellung*, the last of which hugged the top of the reverse slopes. The first line was weakly held, for it took the brunt of the preliminary bombardment and was intended simply as an outpost line to repel patrols and trigger an alert in the event of a serious attack. The second line near the geographical crest of the plateau was the main line of resistance, and close-support units were ready near the third line to launch immediate ripostes against any attackers who broke into the position.

The close-support units were able to shelter from the bombardment inside underground quarries on the northern slopes. The French were aware of the existence of these quarries (known locally as *creutes*), and made arrangements to reduce them with teams

The Chemin des Dames near Hurtebise, in the early months of the war.

Etched into the ground: the German trench system near the present-day Caverne du dragon museum, seen from the air.

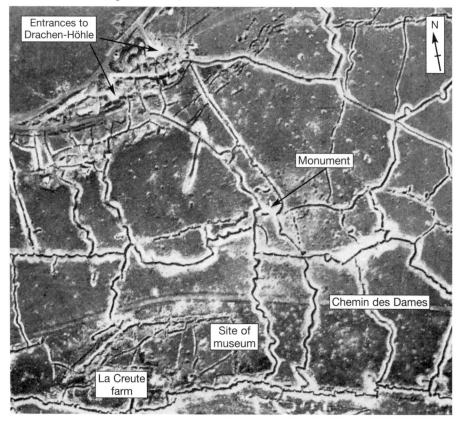

of *nettoyeurs* who were to follow the assault waves and mop up any remaining resistance. But they did not grasp the full extent to which the Germans had enlarged and improved the *creutes* during the past two years. The Germans had also dug tunnels under the Chemin des Dames so they could move troops forward under cover to their first or second trench-lines.

The onslaught

The artillery preparation began in the first days of April and grew progressively in strength, yet its accuracy was difficult to ensure because observation was hindered by German air superiority and spells of bad weather. By 16 April, when the offensive was unleashed, the shelling had smashed the foremost trenches, but had failed to breach the whole depth of the *I Stellung*, let alone the other positions further behind.

Zero hour was 6.00 am. The sun had just risen, but the sky was overcast and the men had already endured a bitterly cold night after taking up their jumping-off positions. Overburdened with equipment, they struggled to advance across the muddy, shell-pocked ground. At first they stuck close behind the rolling barrage – a moving curtain of artillery fire – but once they ran into German resistance, the barrage rolled on without them in accordance with its inflexible timetable. The infantry lacked enough firepower of their own to break the ensuing deadlock. Rifles clogged with mud were difficult to unjam with numb or frostbitten fingers. Grenades soon ran out. The infantry heavy weapons – such as the 37mm guns, which could have helped reduce pockets of resistance – either lost their crews, were unable to keep up with the advance, or were knocked out.

Above all, it was the German machine-gunners who checked the attack. Emerging from the *creutes* and dugouts in which they had survived the preliminary bombardment, they suddenly opened fire from unsuspected locations. The Germans had long been expecting the attack, and it was they, not the French, who sprang the surprises that day. The complexity of the terrain with its numerous spurs and the existence of multiple exits from the *creutes* enabled the machine-guns to fire into the flanks or even the rear of the assault waves, causing shock and dismay.

Too many French troops accumulated in the fighting area as supporting battalions merged into the ones ahead that had come to a standstill. Controlling the flow of successive units was the responsibility of the field officers, but too many of them were out of action. Three of the four regimental commanders were killed in the first stages of the attack, and both the *groupement* commanders were also out of action – one was wounded after going forward to find out why a regiment had been checked, while the other was captured after straying in front of his own units on the slopes north of Hurtebise farm.

Officers in the crack colonial regiments placed a dangerously high priority on personal leadership, and their divisional commander's own reputation for bravery hardly acted as a restraint. The 2nd Battalion of the *33e régiment d'infanterie coloniale*, for example, lost 29 per cent of its men, but 46 per cent of its *caporaux*, 49 per cent of its NCOs and a staggering 71 per cent of its officers. These disproportionate figures do much to explain why the battalion went astray, and this was all the more unfortunate in that it had a particularly delicate task. It stood at the centre of the division and had to manoeuvre around the rim of the *Trou d'enfer* – the steep-sided 'hell-hole' lying within the right-angle where the forward slopes of the Chemin des Dames changed direction as the plateau abruptly widened out west of Hurtebise farm. The battalion was responsible for ensuring that the impassable *Trou d'enfer* did not cause a permanent gap to open between the division's two *groupements*, but amid the cratered and featureless landscape it inclined too far to the left, leaving them with just a precarious link.

Hurtebise farm before the war.

The patchy nature of German resistance caused other gaps to open within the division and frustrated a general sweep over the plateau. Only at isolated points did units manage to penetrate through the German third line and down the northern slopes. These incursions were soon contained, for the spurs jutting out towards the Ailette valley formed a chain of natural bastions, from where machine-guns covered the slopes in between. Any Frenchmen who ventured down these slopes found themselves under a crossfire from either flank, and they also lacked effective artillery support since they were now out of sight beyond the crest.

Outcome

As the attack broke down in confusion, it became vulnerable to counter-thrusts. Yet these ripostes had to be made at exactly the right moment. If the German close-support units emerged from the *creutes* and tunnels too soon they might be caught in the preliminary bombardment, whereas if they left it too late they risked being trapped inside their lairs as the position overhead was overrun. Tunnel 5 became one such trap when its rear exit on the slopes above the village of Ailles was blocked by French machine-gun fire. Fortunately for the tunnel garrison, it was still linked by an intact telephone line to a *creute*, the *Maiwald-Höhle*, which in turn was able to communicate by signal-lamp with the German artillery batteries 3 km to the north. That evening, a barrage placed around the tunnel entrance forced the French machine-gunners to keep their heads down while the garrison escaped under the cover of dusk.

Marchand's division had been checked as early as 10.00 am. Yet the *19. Reserve-Infanterie-Division*, which held this sector, lacked the strength to retake the lost parts of the *I Stellung*. That required the intervention of the local *Eingreif* unit, the *1. Garde-Infanterie-Division,* but the terrain of the Chemin des Dames hampered both sides. Its steep slopes and the marshy, gas-filled valley of the Ailette in its rear obstructed any attempt to use the *Garde* for an immediate, powerful riposte. So, too, did the scattered nature of the division, the uncertainty about the situation, and the French artillery fire interdicting the roads. Not until the night of 16/17 April did elements of the division start to arrive on the Chemin des Dames plateau.

During the days that followed, the Germans mounted a series of counter-attacks, and by the evening of the 19th had regained nearly the whole of their former third line. Most of the top of the plateau was still in French hands, but it proved a precarious foothold. The Hurtebise sector remained a source of friction for months to come.

WHAT TO SEE

This tour is 14 km long. It is best done on foot, but sticks to the roads up to Point F so the first part can be driven if wished. We shall begin by descending the southern face of the Chemin des Dames to see how formidable the slopes appeared to the French attackers. From the car park at the Caverne du dragon museum, walk 400 metres eastwards along the D18 CD to the crossroads in front of Hurtebise farm, and then turn right on to the unsignposted road that snakes its way down into the valley. After 1.25 km the road bends round to the left and loops back on itself. You have come to the lost village of La Vallée Foulon.

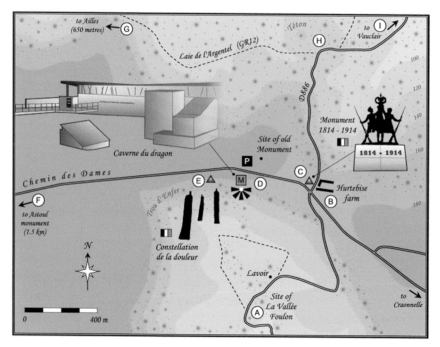

Tour I: Hurtebise.

Point A: La Vallée Foulon

Barely anything remains of the destroyed village today, but the old laundry pool can still be seen at its northern tip. On the eve of the attack, the French front line passed through La Vallée Foulon. From certain points nearby, you can see the roof of the Caverne du dragon museum 600 metres to the north, where the German front line ran along the edge of the plateau. The French position was completely dominated: the difference in elevation between the two sides was 75 metres.

Point B: Hurtebise farm

Walk back up the road to Hurtebise. The farm was destroyed during the war, but has been rebuilt in the same style and at the same spot. A couple of plaques adorn the wall next to the crossroads. One records an action in May 1940 involving elements of *Colonel* Charles de Gaulle's armoured division. The other is inscribed: 'To the glory of the *4e régiment de zouaves*, victor in the actions of 1914 and 1917 against the German Imperial Guard at Hurtebise farm.'

Hurtebise was one of the pockets of German resistance that frustrated the attack on 16 April 1917. The French eventually captured the ruined farm, only to lose it a week later to a surprise attack by the *1. Garde-Regiment zu Fuß* on the morning of the 25th. To restore the situation, a company of the *4e zouaves* – part of the crack *38e division* – launched a counter-attack. As the *zouaves* closed in, a wounded German soldier surrendered and handed some cigarettes to *Lieutenant* Ducros. The *lieutenant* casually distributed them among his comrades, ignoring the machine-gun fire and exploding grenades. His coolness impressed the German prisoner. 'We're the 1st Regiment of the Guard,' the man is reported to have said. 'We're the German élite. But you're better.' Hurtebise farm was soon back in French hands, and the *4e zouaves* earned their fourth citation in army orders.

Point C: Monument

Outside the farm is a monument to the French troops who fought here. Inaugurated in 1927, it shows a soldier of the First World War alongside his predecessor in Napoleon's army – one of the young conscripts known as the *Marie-Louises*. 'To the valour of French youth' reads the inscription. '*Marie-Louise* of 1814, *Bleus* of 1914, united in one and the same glory.' In 1814, Hurtebise was the focal point of the Battle of

ESE

Hurtebise farm

Chemin des Dames

The rebuilt farm of Hurtebise, seen from where the Monument once stood.

Post marking the site of the destroyed Monument, c.1919.

Craonne, when Napoleon was defending France from invasion. Attacking westwards along the crest of the Chemin des Dames, he eventually drove back 18,000 Russian troops who were blocking the narrow saddle of high ground at the farm.

The monument is the work of the sculptor Maxime Réal del Sarte. He himself was a veteran of the war, in which he won the *Médaille militaire* and lost part of his left arm. His design is not entirely accurate: the style of tunic on the statue of the *Marie-Louise* was officially replaced in 1812, and the other soldier belongs to the period after the colourful uniform of 1914 had given way to the plainer *bleu horizon* and the steel helmet.

An earlier monument to Napoleon's victory used to stand in the fields 350 metres west of Hurtebise. It was a stone obelisk, erected in 1904 and inaugurated on the centenary of the battle in March 1914. Just six months later it was blown up by German combat engineers on 24 September in order to deprive the French artillery of an aiming point. Yet the mound on which it had stood remained tactically important. This hump continued to be referred to as the *Monument,* and in the spring and summer of 1917 was one of the points of friction that both sides needed to secure their precarious hold on top of the plateau. It repeatedly changed hands until the French *151e division* conquered the area in a carefully planned attack on 31 August.

Point D: Caverne du dragon

Walk westwards along the D18 CD to the Caverne du dragon. This is the most famous of all the underground quarries on the Chemin des Dames, and has been turned into a museum. We shall remain above ground, for the interior of the cavern forms a separate visit and is described in Stop 12. At the southern edge of the road stand three monuments in a row. The two on the right are covered in Stop 12. The other is a memorial to the *4e zouaves*, who distinguished themselves by holding the nearby farm of La Creute during the First Battle of the Aisne in September 1914. (The farm was never rebuilt after the war.)

In April 1917, the Caverne du dragon sheltered some of the German troops during the bombardment that preceded the offensive. Parts of the quarry collapsed under the impact of the shells, but the garrison managed to clear an exit to the first line. Almost every hour a nervous outpost shouted *Der Franzmann kommt!* – 'The French are coming!' – but it was only a false alarm. On the morning of the 16th the shout was heard once again, and this time was accompanied by the sound of machine-guns and hand-grenades. The garrison hurriedly manned the trenches outside and repelled a frontal attack, but became exposed when the French broke into the positions on either side. 'We were therefore a little fortress in ourselves,' noted the garrison commander. Towards noon his men had to abandon the last part of the first line, and soon afterwards the only surviving entrance to the cavern from that line was smashed. The Germans still held the bulk of the cavern, but the southern part was uninhabitable and, with the exits now blocked, they could no longer see into the valley to the south.

Point E: Constellation de la douleur

On the hillside to the west of the Caverne du dragon is a memorial known as the 'Constellation of grief'. Inaugurated in 2007, it consists of nine elongated figures made from pieces of charred wood and commemorates the *tirailleurs sénégalais*, the Black African soldiers who fought and died in French service.

The Senegalese were treated as a pool of additional manpower, but there had been opposition to using them in combat roles and they were not regarded as a priority for equipment. The *48e bataillon*, for example, had no grenades and only a few automatic rifles. 'In short,' noted the battalion war diary, 'the *tirailleurs* have just a few rounds, their bayonet, and their *coupe-coupe* [a weapon similar to a machete]. The rifles are in too bad a state of maintenance to be used properly.'

The Senegalese were particularly vulnerable to the cold, as is shown by the losses of the *58e régiment d'infanterie coloniale*. Between 15 and 19 April, 16 per cent of the regiment's black soldiers were evacuated sick, compared to under 1 per cent of the European other ranks. A further 22 per cent of the black men were missing, compared to fewer than 6 per cent of the European other ranks. (The proportion of killed and wounded was similar for both the blacks and the Europeans, at around 23 per cent.) By the time the regiment was relieved on 18 April, its men were wrecks. 'The *tirailleurs* are in an indescribable state of physical degradation', reported the regiment's war diary, 'and the Europeans absolutely exhausted. Everyone, without exception, is shambling along.'

Point F: Astoul monument

As you walk further west along the D18 CD, the narrow saddle of high ground abruptly opens out to your left into the plateau de Paissy. When you come to Le Poteau d'Ailles farm, you are at the western edge of Marchand's sector. Continue for another 850 metres, into the sector of the *15e division d'infanterie coloniale*. At the roadside on your right is a monument to a fallen French officer of a Senegalese battalion. The inscription reads: 'In memory of our dearly beloved son, *Sous-lieutenant* Louis Astoul of the *70e sénégalais*, who fell gloriously in this area at the age of 24 during the assault of 16 April 1917, and in memory of his comrades.'

On the eve of the attack, the French front line at this point lay close to the roadway of the Chemin des Dames. The *70e bataillon de tirailleurs sénégalais* gained 700 metres of ground before being checked by machine-gun fire near a trench-line at the northern edge of the plateau. According to Astoul's citation, he 'led his *section* with a remarkable vivacity to assault the German positions, directing his men as if on an exercise, up until the moment when he was mortally wounded.' His remains were never found.

Point G: Ailles

Retrace your steps 150 metres eastwards along the D18 CD and then turn left on to the unsignposted track leading northwards across the fields. This is the route of the GR12 long-distance footpath. Continue along it over the crest of the plateau as far as the barn, and then turn right on to the track heading due east. At the end of the track, turn left on to the road that gently descends to the tree-covered slopes of the Ailette valley. The road veers to the right once it has entered the forest, and after another 550 metres reaches a monument to the lost village of Ailles.

Ailles had fewer than 120 inhabitants before the war, and was destroyed during the bombardments of 1917. It was never rebuilt, and plans to mark its site with a chapel or even a modest calvary came to nothing. The monument you see today was the result of a campaign launched by the *Touring-club de France* in 1932 to preserve the memory of villages that had been wiped out by the war. The inscription reads simply: 'Here stood Ailles, destroyed in 1914–1918 during the German invasion.' (The village actually stood 200 metres further east.) The

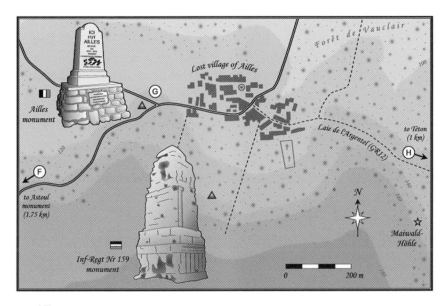

Ailles.

pattern below the inscription is meant to show the village layout, and the base of the monument consists of stones taken from the ruins.

A second monument is hidden in the forest 350 metres to the south-east. You are advised not to try to find it, as it lies deep inside and lacks an access path. It commemorates a German unit, *Infanterie-Regiment Nr 159*, which fought in this sector during the First Battle of the Aisne in 1914 and remained here until October 1915. The regiment established a military cemetery for its fallen immediately outside Ailles, and inaugurated its monument on 17 September 1915, shortly before it left the Chemin des Dames and exactly a year after it had made its first attack in this vicinity. The subsequent bombardments left the monument badly damaged. Almost all of the inscriptions have been destroyed, and the battered core lacks the eagle that was once perched on top.

Point H: *Téton*
From the 'Here stood Ailles' monument, take the road to the east signposted for Chermizy. At the bend 300 metres further on, turn right on to the track through the forest – you will see a sign with its name, the

Laie de l'Argentel. The track passes along the lower slopes of the Chemin des Dames and joins the D886 700 metres north of Hurtebise farm. Hidden amidst the trees immediately north-west of this junction is a rounded hill, which was known to the French as the *Téton* since it was shaped like a breast.

The *Téton* was high enough, and lay sufficiently far back in the Ailette valley, to enfilade the northern slopes of the Chemin des Dames in the entire sector attacked by Marchand's division. Nowadays, the hill and the whole of its surroundings are covered in trees, but on 16 April 1917 several large clearings existed in the forest and the German detachments holding the hill had some good fields of fire. When elements of the *33e régiment d'infanterie coloniale* broke through near Hurtebise farm, they were checked towards 8.30 am at the edge of a clearing on the eastern side of the *Téton*. What happened next was typical of the problems that occurred wherever fractions of Marchand's division managed to penetrate through the *I Stellung* into the Ailette valley. The remnants of the group near the *Téton* were dangerously exposed in front of the rest of the division, and deprived of effective artillery support since they had passed beyond the crest of the Chemin des Dames. Almost cut off by German fire, and with the forest making it impossible to communicate with signal lamps, they waited in vain for reinforcements. After spending more than six hours under machine-gun fire and artillery bombardment, they had to fall back.

Point I: Vauclair abbey

From the *Téton*, turn left on to the D886, and follow it for 1 km until you come to the abbey of Vauclair. Most of the abbey was already in ruins by 1914, but some parts – including the gatehouse on the western side of the grounds and the lay-brothers' massive building – were destroyed during the war. As you wander around the grounds, you will spot scars left by bullets or shells in the stonework. The seventeenth-century dovecot used to be an octagonal structure covered with a roof, but three of the eight sides were smashed by the bombardments. From Vauclair, which marks the end of the tour, you can return to the Chemin des Dames by heading south along the D886.

Tour II
Tank Assault
16 April 1917

Nivelle's onslaught fell not only on the Chemin des Dames. Further to the right, the *5e armée* extended the attack front 25 km south-eastwards to the vicinity of Reims. In this tour we shall visit the low-lying plains in the centre of the *5e armée*, where it had the support of a massed array of tanks. Never before had the French used tanks, and even the British, who had first committed theirs on the Somme in September 1916, had only ever done so in limited numbers. On 16 April 1917, the French sent as many as 121 into action in the first large-scale tank attack in history.

WHAT HAPPENED
The idea of using an armoured vehicle to break the deadlock of the Western Front was pursued simultaneously in both France and Britain. Yet support for the tank was far from universal, and progress was hampered by bureaucracy and business rivalries. Instead of producing a single type of tank, the Allies worked separately, and even within

Baptism of fire: a Schneider tank in action on 16 April 1917.

France two designs – the Schneider and the Saint-Chamond – were developed by different firms.

The tanks used on the first day of the Nivelle offensive were Schneiders. They looked like an iron rhinoceros: a rectangular block of brute force, 6 metres long, 2 metres wide, and 2.40 metres high, with a front that sloped upwards and tapered to end in a horn-like spur. The armour was up to 17mm thick, and proof against bullets. The crew of six entered and left through a double-door at the back, but had to endure hot, cramped and noisy conditions inside and became stupefied by exhaustion and petrol fumes.

The Schneider weighed 13.5 tonnes, yet had just a 60 horsepower engine and its speed over undulating terrain was a paltry 2–4 km an hour – no faster than an infantryman. In contrast, a modern British tank, the Challenger 2, is over four-and-a-half times as heavy, but has an engine twenty times as powerful, enabling it to move at around 40 km an hour across country.

The Schneider's weaponry consisted of two Hotchkiss machine-guns in cupolas on the sides of the hull, and a 75mm mortar. The mortar had a maximum effective range of 600 metres and was mounted in a corner of the hull rather than in a turret, so its arc of fire was only 20 degrees. But firepower was of limited importance. The real effectiveness of the tank lay in its psychological impact and in its ability to keep moving forward amidst a hail of bullets that would have cut down waves of infantry.

The plan

Two armoured *groupements*, or battalions, were committed to the attack. In this tour we shall focus on the larger of the two, *Groupement Bossut*, which was entrusted with the main effort immediately north of the Aisne. The area chosen for its intervention was the 2-km wide corridor between the river and its tributary, the Miette. The terrain was open and gently undulating, with just a handful of woods, but was dominated by high ground on all sides. Any movement could be spotted by German observers on the Chemin des Dames to the north-west, on the height at Prouvais in the north-east, and on Hill 108 and Mont de Sapigneul south of the Aisne.

The sector between the Aisne and the Miette was held by two infantry regiments of the Bavarian *5. Reserve-Infanterie-Division*. The

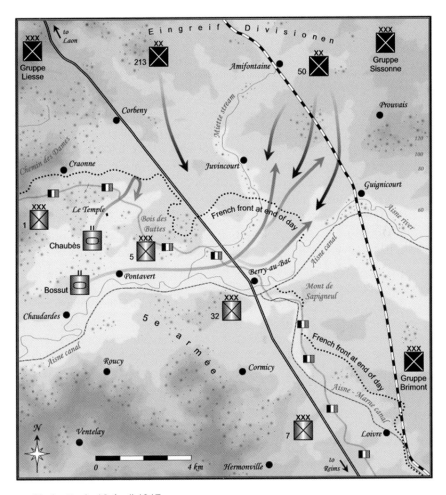

Tank attack, 16 April 1917.

defensive zone consisted of several positions arrayed 2 or 3 km behind one another: the *I Stellung,* the *Artillerie-Schutzstellung* to protect the battery emplacements, then the *II Stellung* and, even further to the rear, the beginnings of a *III Stellung.*

The Germans had taken the precaution of widening the trenches of the *I Stellung.* This frustrated any notion of using tanks to spearhead a surprise attack and made it necessary to relegate them to the role of a supporting arm. The infantry would have to conquer the crust of the

German defences in the wake of the bombardment, and only then – after passages had been created through the *I Stellung* and the *Artillerie-Schutzstellung* – would the tanks come forward and join the second phase of the attack by assaulting the rearmost German positions. These rearward positions lay more than 5 km behind the front line and were too distant to be devastated by the preliminary bombardment. The intervention of the tanks was intended to supplement the limited effects of the long-range shelling and maintain the attack's momentum by dispensing with the fatal pause that normally ensued when guns and ammunition had to be laboriously brought forward to support a renewed advance. The role of the French armour was spelled out by its name: the *Artillerie spéciale,* or *Artillerie d'assaut (AS)*.

Berry-au-Bac, 16 April 1917.

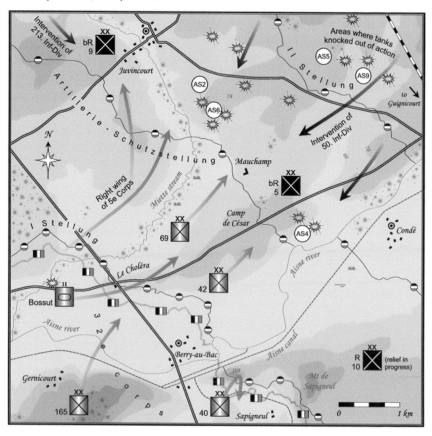

The infantry assigned to attack this sector were from the *32e corps*. Three divisions stood side-by-side astride the Aisne. Two of them – the *69e division* on the left and the *42e* in the centre – were north of the river. The righthand division, the *40e*, would assault Hill 108 and Mont de Sapigneul on the south bank. In support was the *165e division*, which had been attached to the corps from the army reserve and was to follow the advance on the north bank.

Into action

The infantry went over the top at 6.00 am on 16 April. The *I Stellung* quickly fell. The artillery preparation had crushed the first two trench-lines, and in the sector between the Aisne and the Miette the attack caught both of the Bavarian regiments while they were in the process of relieving their foremost battalion. Large numbers of prisoners were taken, yet isolated pockets of resistance had to be mopped up and progress became increasingly difficult. As the morning mist lifted, the German artillery barrage intensified and numerous machine-guns came into action. The deep defensive zones studded with strongpoints or machine-gun nests enabled even skeletal units to hold up the advance. The further the French infantry pushed in the area between the Aisne and the Miette, the more exposed they became on either flank, where the neighbouring units had been unable to keep pace.

By mid-morning, the attack had lost its momentum after struggling through the *Artillerie-Schutzstellung*. The result was stalemate: the German field batteries were now exposed by the loss of their covering position, but the French infantry had been checked by exhaustion, casualties and hostile fire. Now was the time for the tanks to intervene and renew the impetus. *Groupement Bossut* contained five armoured *groupes*, each of which had a total of sixteen tanks organized into four batteries. After moving forward in column, the *groupes* were meant to deploy into a line 3.5 km long, extending from the Miette at Juvincourt to the Aisne near Condé. They were supposed to reach this line in time to attack the *II Stellung* at 10.00 am, but as a result of congestion they arrived only between 12.00 in the north and 3.00 pm in the south. Even without these delays, it would have proved impossible to coordinate them on such a wide front with the inadequate means of communication available in 1917. Instead of making a general attack, the five *groupes* ended up fighting piecemeal actions.

The deepest penetration was made by *AS5* in the centre. Nine of its tanks managed to pass beyond the *II Stellung*, and one of them actually reconnoitred as far as the Laon–Reims railway line, 6 km behind the former German front, before being immobilized by a shell as it returned. The *groupe* was too isolated and short of petrol to continue, for the French infantry had come to a standstill some 2 km in the rear. Its tanks cruised around to avoid artillery fire, and those that remained mobile pulled back in the evening.

Striking back

Behind the Bavarians stood two fresh units, the *50.* and *213. Infanterie-Divisionen*. They were specially trained as *Eingreif-Divisionen*: rapid intervention units with the mission of countering any break-in before the attackers could consolidate their gains. Parts of these divisions had been placed as far forward as the *II Stellung* so they could make immediate counter-thrusts. The remaining elements were released in mid-morning to make a more powerful riposte on either side of the Miette. The *213. Infanterie-Division* had only a limited effect, but the impact of the *50. Infanterie-Division* further south was more substantial. Here, between the Aisne and the Miette, the French came under a series of blows throughout the day – at first localized and small in scale as the Bavarians threw in their reserves and the leading elements of the *50. Infanterie-Division* intervened, but building up to a general attack by the remaining four battalions of the division in the afternoon. This general attack was checked after making modest gains, yet reconquering the whole of a position regardless of cost was not part of German doctrine. The intervention of the *Eingreif-Division* had achieved its primary purpose by stabilizing the situation and re-establishing a cohesive front.

Counting the cost

That evening the surviving tanks withdrew from the battlefield. Three in every five of Bossut's machines had either ditched, broken down or been knocked out by shells. The other armoured *groupement* sent into action that day suffered a disaster after it became bottled up in no man's land, where it remained exposed to artillery fire for the entire day. In the two *groupements* combined, one-quarter of the officers and men committed to the attack were killed, wounded, or missing, and the dead included Bossut himself.

The superficial impression is one of failure. Yet the tanks were just one element in a general offensive, and it was the offensive as a whole that had miscarried. If the Chemin des Dames and its observation points had fallen as planned in the opening hours, the tanks would have been less exposed in the plains to artillery fire. Even under these adverse conditions, they had some success, above all in blunting the intervention of the *50. Infanterie-Division*. They were mobile machine-gun platforms invulnerable to bullets, and they easily checked infantry attacking across open ground in their presence. A German soldier described his sense of helplessness when four tanks appeared just 150 metres from him:

It took our breath away. Slowly but surely the things came clattering up. What now? We had only our rifles and lacked any effective weapons with which to fight. None of us thought of running away, yet what were we to do?

Only artillery could deal with a tank. More than one in three of Bossut's tanks was knocked out by German guns – often by a shell exploding nearby rather than by a direct hit. Even more alarming was the ease with which these stricken tanks caught fire: in 69 per cent of cases they went up in flames. (A raft of measures was subsequently taken to address this problem, such as increasing the ventilation and moving the location of the petrol tank.)

The experience at Berry-au-Bac was costly but instructive. The tanks needed to be shielded as much as possible from artillery fire and integrated more closely with the other arms. In accordance with the doctrine in force at the time of the attack, the infantry and armour had advanced in succession towards their shared objectives. They provided mutual support, but one awaited the other only if unable to progress further on its own. The flaws in this concept became obvious under actual battle conditions. 'What a peculiar machine!' thought *Lieutenant* Roger Basteau of the *151e régiment* when he saw a tank for the very first time on the battlefield. 'We had been warned that tanks might intervene during the attack, but we had never seen any of them before and knew nothing of how they might be able to help us.' Individual tanks penetrated deep into the German defensive zone, but their seemingly impressive achievements were ephemeral, for they could not hold conquered ground by themselves. Tanks that stopped moving became sitting targets for artillery, so gains could be consolidated only if infantry support was forthcoming.

The tanks were too slow and mechanically fragile to charge through a defensive system. They had to be set tasks within the limits of their capabilities, and committed on a battlefield specifically chosen with their limitations in mind. Just three weeks later, these crucial lessons bore fruit at Laffaux (Tour III).

WHAT TO SEE
The tour is 35 km long and should be driven. We begin by following the route taken by Bossut's *groupement* from its assembly position 9 km behind the French front line.

Point A: Cuiry
On 10 April, the two armoured *groupements* left their training camp near Compiègne. Transported by railway, they detrained 6 to 8 km south of the Aisne at Courlandon and Ventelay. On successive nights, they then moved by road to assembly positions on the north bank of the Aisne between the villages of Maizy and Cuiry-lès-Chaudardes, where they were hidden amidst the trees from German aircraft.

Since the Aisne offensive was postponed to the 16th, the tank crews had a frustrating wait in makeshift dugouts or abandoned barges on the canal that runs alongside the Aisne. They were not allowed to walk about in the open during the day, and the din from nearby artillery pounding the German positions made it difficult to sleep. At last, on the night of 15/16 April, the two *groupements* set off under cover of darkness for separate attack positions closer to the front line. *Groupement Bossut* moved out at 2.00 am in a single column of eighty-one tanks, and we shall now follow its progress along the Aisne valley. Leave Cuiry from the central crossroads west of the church. Drive 375 metres north-westwards along the *rue du lavoir* until you come to the road junction, then turn right and follow the D925 north-eastwards towards Pontavert.

Point B: Beaurepaire stream
A line of trees 1 km in front of Pontavert marks the course of the Beaurepaire stream. The head of Bossut's column stopped after reaching

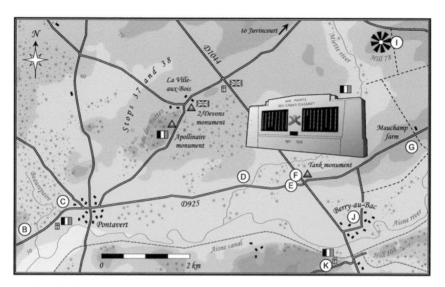

Tour II: Berry-au-Bac.

this point towards 5.30 am. The open ground to the west and south-west of the bridge formed the attack position, where the column could close up and make last-minute preparations before going into action. At 6.30 am, Bossut resumed his move along the D925 towards the front line. At the head of the column was *AS2*, followed by the other *groupes* in the order *AS6, 5, 9, 4*. The entire column was 2 km long. *Commandant* Bossut himself was in the foremost tank, having obtained permission the day before to lead the attack. Progress was slow, for the road was congested with infantry and artillery, and it was around 7.20 am before the tail of the column left the attack position.

Point C: Pontavert

Three hundred metres beyond the Beaurepaire, stop at the French military cemetery of Pontavert. Begun in 1915, it was enlarged after the war as the remains of fallen soldiers were transferred from provisional graves elsewhere. Inside is a monument to the *31e régiment*, which was part of the *5e corps*. The regiment distinguished itself on 16 April 1917 by conquering the German strongpoint of the Bois des Buttes (Stop 38).

Pontavert during the war.

Point D: Miette bridge

Pass through Pontavert village, and pause 3.5 km further on when you reach the bridge over the Miette. Bossut's column reached this point towards 8.00 am. The tanks had been on the move for the past hour-and-a-half, and four of them had already ditched or broken down. They were now under German artillery fire in full daylight, but had to remain in column as they were still hemmed into the narrow corridor of the Aisne valley. One tank was hit after crossing the Miette bridge, and the crews began to suffer their first casualties.

Follow Bossut's route as he continued eastwards along the D925, until you reach the roundabout at the junction with the D1044 (the high-road linking Laon and Reims). On the far side of the roundabout, stop at the car park adjoining the *Monument aux chars d'assaut*.

Point E: Tank monument

The spot chosen for the monument is Bossut's point of departure: it was here that the *groupement* had to cross the foremost German trenches of the *I Stellung*, which had been taken in the first stage of the infantry attack. The monument commemorates the men of the French tank crews who fell during the First World War and was inaugurated in 1922. The sculptor was Maxime Réal del Sarte.

In front of the monument is a memorial stone to *Général de division* Eugène Estienne, a leading figure in the creation of the French armoured force. One of his officers described him as:

> A little, broad-shouldered man, with a round head and piercing eyes, whose look showed intelligence – acuteness even – and much goodwill. He had an unusual tic. With one hand and then the other he would adjust his *képi*, and it rolled and pitched from one ear to the other and from his forehead to the back of his neck.

Two remarks are quoted on the memorial stone, although both of them exaggerate the tank's importance in winning the First World War. The first is a statement made by Estienne in August 1914, when he was a *colonel* commanding the artillery of an infantry division: 'Victory will go to whoever is the first to create an armoured vehicle armed with a cannon and capable of moving over any terrain.' The second remark was made in the German parliament, or *Reichstag*, in October 1918 by the representative of the Supreme Command of the German armies: 'There is no longer any possibility of victory, and the tank is the principal factor in decisively bringing about this state of affairs.'

Note the emblem on the face of the monument, showing a medieval helmet superimposed on two crossed cannon barrels. This was the insignia eventually adopted by the *Artillerie d'assaut*, and symbolizes its combination of armour and firepower. Fixed to the back of the monument is a plaque to the *151e régiment*. It was this regiment – part of the *69e division* – that overran the German defences at this point at the start of the attack.

On the lists of the fallen, the first and most prominent name is that of *Commandant* Louis Bossut. He began his career in the cavalry and gained a reputation as a superb horseman and outstanding leader, full of dash, boldness and enthusiasm. 'Very military, very authoritarian,' read a report from his commanding officer, 'yet has the knack of making himself adored by his men.' He was apparently the inspiration for the character of *Capitaine* de Boëldieu in Jean Renoir's classic 1937 film *La grande illusion*. He insisted on personally leading his *groupement* into battle on 16 April in case the attack failed. 'I do not want the survivors blaming me for the needless deaths of their comrades,' he wrote. 'This fear will be nullified if I lead them in person, and so I agree to give the attack order only if I am the first to march against the enemy.' Bossut was killed in the morning when his tank was hit by a German shell and went up in flames. His body was blown right out of the rear doors by the explosion and was recovered that night. His final citation read: 'After throwing himself into organizing this new arm with all his great gusto as a soldier and dauntless horseman, [he] fell gloriously while leading his tanks in an heroic cavalcade at the last enemy lines.'

This battlefield has immense symbolic importance for the French armoured arm. 'The sacrifice was not in vain', wrote one tank officer in 1918, 'for it gave us a tradition.' Ceremonies are still held at the monument every year. At the entrance to the car park are two examples from a subsequent generation of French armoured fighting vehicles: an AMX-13 light tank and a Panhard EBR armoured reconnaissance vehicle, dating from the 1960s.

Point F: Le Choléra calvary

On the western side of the roundabout stands a calvary with a plaque commemorating *Caporal* Raymond Motte of the *43e régiment*. Motte fell on 17 September 1914, and we will visit his grave later in this tour (Point K). The calvary marks the location of Le Choléra farm. By the time of the attack on 16 April, all that remained of the farm was a whitish patch where the ground had yet to swallow up all the rubble. This point was part of the German first line and dominated the slopes that gently descended across no man's land. The trenches had been crushed by the artillery preparation, and the surrounding area was a chaotic expanse of shell-holes, though the remnants of the high-road between Laon and Reims were still visible.

Two *pistes*, or trails, were meant to have been created to enable Bossut's *groupement* to pass through this cratered ground and across the captured trenches of the *I Stellung*. The task had been assigned to five companies of the *154e régiment*, but German artillery fire forced the men to take cover and only one of the two *pistes* could be made. Bossut's tanks were therefore held up in front of Le Choléra. 'It was a long wait,' wrote *Brigadier* Jean-François Perrette of *AS5*. 'To us, it

Calvary at Le Choléra.

seemed like eternity.' Only at 10.15 am was the leading *groupe, AS2,*
able to continue the advance after passing through the *I Stellung.* By
this stage, all five *groupes* were meant to have deployed and begun the
attack on the *II Stellung,* 4 km further north-east.

Point G: Mauchamp farm

From Le Choléra, follow the progress of the French attack by driving north-eastwards along the D925 towards Guignicourt. The road follows the shallow crest in between the Aisne and Miette valleys, and commands views of much of the battlefield. It was on this rising ground, covered by the watercourses on three sides, that Julius Caesar established a camp during his campaign against the *Belgae* in 57 BC. Midway to Guignicourt you will come to Mauchamp farm, which occupies the summit of the crest at the point where it was crossed by the *Artillerie-Schutzstellung*. This strong position was taken in the morning by the *42e division*, but the southernmost armoured *groupe*, *AS4*, was checked when it tried to push further east after its belated arrival in the afternoon. The farm was rebuilt here after the war, but originally stood 850 metres further north-west.

Point H: Juvincourt

Continue north-eastwards along the D925 for another 2.75 km, up to the junction with the D62 at the western outskirts of Guignicourt. Turn left on to the D62 and follow it north-westwards to Juvincourt. This village in the Miette valley was crucial to the outcome of the battle. By holding it, the Germans prevented the *5e* and *32e corps* on either bank of the stream from supporting each other adequately. They also deprived Bossut's *groupement* of the secure western flank it needed at the point where a bend in the stream opened up the hitherto constricted corridor between the Miette and the Aisne into a swathe of land 4 km wide. The deeper the tanks penetrated into this zone, the more vulnerable they became to enfilade fire.

Point I: Hill 78

For the best views over the battlefield, park your car at Juvincourt and walk back along the D62. After 1.5 km, turn right along the unsignposted track leading southwards across the fields. Follow it for 200 metres until you reach the top of the rising ground. This is Hill 78, though the elevation marked on some maps is 77 metres.

From here, you have views in all directions. To the east-north-east is the wooded hill of Prouvais, Bossut's objective for the day. The line of trees in the middle distance shows the course of the motorway that cuts across the battlefield: it marks the approximate location of the *II*

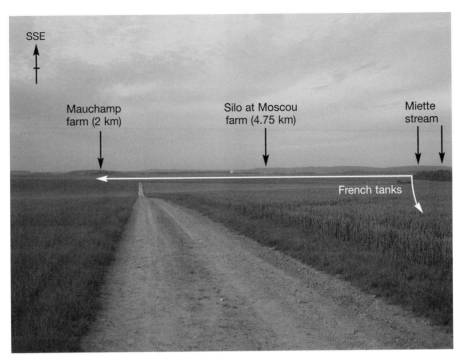

Tank country: the open, rolling terrain seen from Hill 78.

Stellung, 1 km east of where you are standing. To the south is Mauchamp farm, in its new location alongside the D925. The massive silo in the Aisne valley further to your right adjoins Moscou farm, 900 metres south of Berry-au-Bac. To the west you can see the Chemin des Dames on the horizon. Nestled in the Miette valley to the north-west is the village of Juvincourt with its white water-tower.

The action on Hill 78 unfolded during the course of the afternoon. The leading tank *groupe*, *AS2*, was earmarked to deploy at the northern end of the attack front. Followed by *AS6*, it crossed the *Artillerie-Schutzstellung* near the Miette around 11.30 am. Shortly after noon, five of its tanks reached the top of the hill. For half-an-hour they remained here, moving around so as not to offer a sitting target, and vainly waited for the infantry to join them. (The signal to summon the infantry forward was a simple one: the tank crews simply opened their rear doors, the inside of which had been painted white.)

Eventually, the tanks gave up waiting and tried to advance on their own. But the terrain north of the hill was dangerously exposed. Seven tanks were now in the area (two more had arrived), but they were under fire from German guns from several directions. Four of them were knocked out by shells, and at 2.00 pm the three survivors withdrew to Hill 78. A German soldier later passed the burned-out wrecks:

> It was a horrifying sight. The bodies of the crews had been smashed and burnt. The crew of one tank had fled from it in flames and, being drenched in fuel, had died an agonizing death. We had already seen many sights, but this one was too dreadful, especially as the bodies were bloated from the unusual heat, which made them twitch and move.

Following this setback, thirteen tanks from *AS2* and *AS6* assembled in a line behind the cover of Hill 78. When elements of the *50. Infanterie-Division* intervened in the action towards 2.30 pm, the tanks moved on to the crest of Hill 78, dislocated the attack with their fire, and then fell back behind the hill.

It was clear that any renewed advance by the tanks would be pointless in the absence of infantry support. The *69e division* (the northern wing of the *32e corps*) was too weary and disorganized to progress further without reinforcement. Too many of its officers had become casualties. A reserve unit – the *165e division* – was therefore placed at the division's disposal for a renewed attack on a broad front that evening. By now, the tanks were short of petrol and unable to do more than occupy Hill 78 in order to protect the western flank of the attack. They set off towards 5.20 pm, followed by elements of the *151e* and *155e régiments*. Unlike their earlier advances, the tanks had infantry support, yet they were again checked by artillery fire once they reached the crest of the hill. By 6.00 pm the attack had come to a standstill and one of the tanks was ablaze. This final, belated push had ended in stalemate.

Point J: Berry-au-Bac

Retrieve your car and return to the Tank monument at Le Choléra. At the roundabout in front of the monument, take the turning on to the

The Aisne river at Berry-au-Bac before the war.

D1044 signposted for Reims and drive the 1.5 km into Berry-au-Bac. You will find a car park behind the *mairie* in the centre of the town.

Berry-au-Bac has long been an important crossing point of the Aisne, lying as it does on the direct route between Laon and Reims. A plaque on the bridge carrying the D1044 over the river commemorates Napoleon's cavalrymen who seized the crossing for him in 1814, two days before the Battle of Craonne. It was here, too, that Julius Caesar crossed the Aisne in 57 BC, during his campaign against the *Belgae*.

By April 1917 Berry-au-Bac had already been reduced to ruins, for it lay just 300 metres behind the French front line, in low ground that was particularly exposed to German observation from Hill 108 on the southern side of the Aisne. 'It was the most awful death-trap in existence,' wrote one soldier. The Aisne caused additional problems, since it was 50 metres wide and regularly flooded the valley in winter. 'We are living in the water like frogs', wrote a *capitaine* in December 1915, 'and our only way of getting out of it is to lie on our beds, which are hung inside our shelters.' The *capitaine* in question was serving with the *33e régiment* north of Berry-au-Bac. His name was Charles de Gaulle.

Ruins of Berry-au-Bac church in August 1916.

As the war progressed, the French had to build additional bridges over the Aisne and the canal that ran parallel to it. They also began to use the canal as a transport artery, moving supplies forward by boat and evacuating wounded men westwards. Thick ice interrupted these movements during the harsh winter of 1916/17.

Point K: French military cemetery

Drive out of Berry-au-Bac along the D1044, heading south-eastwards across the Aisne and then the lateral canal. One hundred metres beyond the canal, turn right on to the D1140 (signposted for Gernicourt and the military cemetery of Berry-au-Bac). Drive up the hill, and you will see the cemetery on your right after 200 metres.

The cemetery was created in 1919 and contains the remains of almost 4,000 men. Among them is the commander of one of Bossut's armoured *groupes*, *Capitaine* Jean Pardon of *AS2*, who is buried in Grave 966. He was mortally wounded by a shell-burst early in the afternoon while abandoning a broken-down tank south of Hill 78. Grave 1685 is that of *Caporal* Motte, whose memorial we saw at Point F. *Sergent* Paul Gobron (Grave 1633) belonged to the *332e régiment*, one of the units of the *42e division*, and fell on 16 April 1917. By sheer coincidence, he was killed less than 10 km from his birthplace: you will find his name on the local war memorial at the village of Berméricourt, a short drive to the south-east (Stop 44).

A memorial inside the cemetery remembers the fallen men of an engineer unit, Company 19/3 of the *2e régiment du génie*. In 1916, the company spent over five months, from the end of May to early November, engaged in mine warfare at Hill 108 (Stop 39). During that period, two of its officers and thirty-nine other ranks were killed. Some are buried within the cemetery, but others remain entombed inside Hill 108.

Optional visit
The German military cemetery of Veslud (Stop 22) contains a monument to the *50. Infanterie-Division*, one of the *Eingreif-Divisionen* that intervened in the Berry-au-Bac sector on 16 April.

The French military cemetery at Berry-au-Bac, shortly after its creation.

Tour III
Laffaux

5–6 May 1917

Guarding the western gateway of the Chemin des Dames is a natural bastion known as the moulin de Laffaux. It forms the central summit of an intricate arm of high ground that extends the Chemin des Dames plateau towards Soissons. The actual *moulin*, an old windmill, disappeared long before the First World War, leaving just a road hub and a handful of buildings, yet this minor locality was militarily important because of its commanding position. Surrounded by valleys on four sides, it straddled the historic invasion route of the N2, the great *chaussée* leading south-westwards to Paris.

The moulin de Laffaux was an obvious target for a French attack. Though naturally strong, the position was vulnerable to being pinched out since it formed a salient. By the start of May, the German front line at this point was bent back at an angle of 120 degrees, forming the so-called *Laffaux-Ecke*, a 'corner' that could be enfiladed by artillery from both west and south.

The Laffaux sector had already been attacked on 16 April at the start of the Nivelle offensive, but the unit involved, the *1er corps d'armée colonial*, had made only limited progress. The corps managed to add slightly to its gains during the days that followed, and established a foothold on the western edge of the high ground by occupying the ruins of Laffaux village. But the central stronghold of the moulin de Laffaux was still in German hands. Cracking this position would require a major set-piece attack.

WHAT HAPPENED

The capture of the moulin de Laffaux was just one in a string of French attacks mounted along the Chemin des Dames on 5 May. The plan at the western end of the plateau was to launch a converging attack with two prongs formed by the *1er corps d'armée colonial* in the west and the

6e corps in the east. They were linked by the *37e corps*, whose *158e division* would make a secondary attack.

In the *1er corps d'armée colonial*, one of the two divisions was so worn out that it was replaced with a specially constituted unit, a *division provisoire* commanded by *Général de brigade* Charles Brécard. This was the division entrusted with taking the moulin de Laffaux, and it was composed of three dismounted *cuirassier* regiments.

Cuirassiers were élite, heavy cavalrymen. They could trace their regimental origins back to the 1600s and many of their officers had an equally distinguished personal lineage, as is clear from their unmistakably aristocratic names. Among them was Adrien de Hauteclocque, who was serving with his eldest son Guy in the *11e cuirassiers à pied*. (A younger son, Philippe, was still too young to fight, but would win fame in the Second World War under the *nom de guerre* of *Général* Leclerc.)

Moulin de Laffaux, 5 May 1917.

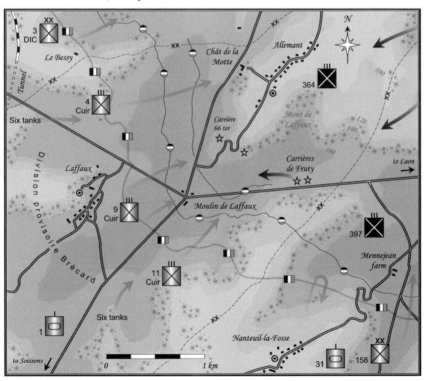

In 1914, the *cuirassiers* had ridden off to war wearing their traditional plates of armour, but by the end of that year they were providing detachments to serve in the trenches and in 1916 they were re-equipped as infantry units. Laffaux was the first time that the dismounted *cuirassier* regiments took part in a large-scale attack. Brécard's division was sandwiched between the *3e division d'infanterie coloniale* to the north and the *158e division* to the south-east. Its general objective lay 2.5 km away, at the north-eastern end of Allemant village. To reach this line, the division would advance in stages, gaining three intermediate objectives one after the other. These intermediate objectives were the first and second German lines, and the edge of the plateau above the Allemant basin. The three regiments of Brécard's division were drawn up side-by-side. The *9e régiment* was in the centre, tasked with capturing the moulin de Laffaux, with the *4e* on its left flank, and the *11e* on its right. Each regiment had three battalions: one to spearhead the attack, one in support and one in reserve.

Descending directly into the Allemant basin would be dangerous. It lay just 700 metres behind the moulin de Laffaux, and the Germans had placed reserves under the cover of its steep slopes, ready for immediate counter-thrusts. The solution that the French planners devised was an encircling attack to surround Allemant and the various quarries and dugouts that lay south-west of the village. The centre was not to enter the basin until all three regiments had conquered the semi-circular rim of high ground that dominated it. Yet in order to reach that rim, each regiment had to overcome a major obstacle: the moulin de Laffaux in the centre, the Château de la Motte in the north, and the quarries known as the carrières de Fruty in the east. A check at any one of these three points would compromise the attack as a whole.

Brécard's division had the support of a *groupe* of fifteen Schneider tanks. The *groupe (AS1)* kept three tanks in reserve and assigned each of its remaining three batteries to support a *cuirassier* regiment. It was the second time in three weeks that the French used tanks in action, and valuable lessons had been learned from their debut on 16 April (Tour II). Instead of making a long approach march under artillery fire, the tanks were now placed in attack positions just 1 km behind the front line, concealed on the slopes below the plateau. The infantry and armour were coordinated more closely, and each tank was accompanied by a group of three *chasseurs à pied* specially trained to aid its progress and liaise between it and the *cuirassiers*.

Dawn attack

The attack was launched at 4.45 am on the 5th. Mist and smoke shrouded the plateau as the *cuirassiers* advanced behind a rolling barrage. They overran the German first line, which was sited slightly in front of the crest of the plateau and had taken the brunt of the artillery preparation, but found progress more difficult the deeper they penetrated. The German defensive system consisted of a succession of lines, studded with formidable concrete dugouts that had to be reduced one-by-one with grenades. Concealed machine-gun nests were scattered across the shell-pocked terrain, and reserves were waiting close at hand in the shelter of the Allemant ravine.

By 6.00 am, the attack had begun to falter. The *cuirassiers* had overrun the German first line and parts of the second, but still had to mop up the remaining defenders, which took longer than expected. In the centre, for example, a pocket of resistance at the moulin de Laffaux held out until mid-morning, even though the *9e régiment* had already penetrated 150 metres beyond it. Brécard's division had ceased to make a general advance, and was now fighting a series of small-scale actions.

Progress was eased for a while by the intervention of the tanks. Having set off at zero hour behind the spearhead battalions, they joined the assault waves on the plateau and began breaching belts of wire, dealing with strongpoints and machine-gun nests, and breaking up some German counter-thrusts. *Lieutenant* Pierre Lestringuez watched from one tank as two others knocked out a concrete stronghold:

> One of them manoeuvred ponderously around a point that I could not see. It fell back and advanced, as if seeking a favourable position. Then its cannon jerked and there was a flash of light, followed by an immediate explosion at point-blank range. A couple of shots came from the second tank, one after the other, with two similar flashes. It was like kicking an ant-hill: Boches emerged from every hole, blackened and haggard, with their arms raised, without rifles or equipment.

But the primitive tanks were ponderous and mechanically fragile, and were confined to the plateau since they were unable to venture down the steep slopes into the Allemant basin. Of *AS1*'s fifteen tanks, five ditched or broke down. The crews grew exhausted after four or five hours spent cooped up inside their vehicles. By mid-morning they regarded their mission as complete and withdrew from the battle rather than remain longer than necessary on the exposed plateau, where they risked being hit by artillery fire.

In the absence of the tanks, the *cuirassiers* now had to fight and manoeuvre their own way forward, but were overburdened with equipment and sapped by the intense heat of the day. Artillery support was inadequate because of the difficulties in keeping the gunners informed of the progress of the attack, and in indicating precise targets. Most of the German second line lay behind the shallow crest of the plateau and was hidden from ground-based artillery observers.

The devastation at the moulin de Laffaux.

Stalled advance

By 9.00 am, the attack had come to a standstill practically everywhere. The biggest stumbling block was on the far right wing, where the *11e régiment* had been checked by enfilade fire. The *cuirassiers* were out on a limb, for the divisions on either flank had failed to keep pace. Brécard initially intended to wait until the situation became clearer before launching a second push later that day, but after being prodded by a message from his army corps he changed his mind and ordered the attack to resume at 11.00 am.

Improvising a new attack with units already engaged was fraught with difficulties. The rear headquarters were closely linked to each other, but had no reliable means of communicating with the *cuirassier* squadrons in the combat zone. Telephone lines tended to be cut by shelling, and pigeons were vulnerable to gas. Flares and other optical signals could be difficult to see amidst the dust and smoke, so messages had to be carried by chains of runners, who were simply too slow. In the *4e régiment*, for example, it was 10.35 am before the order to resume the attack reached the *colonel*, and his spearhead battalion received it only at 12.30 pm – a full ninety minutes after the intended jumping-off time.

Brécard postponed the attack to 6.00 pm, but was again frustrated by the slow communications. Before the spearhead battalions could be informed of the postponement, they belatedly went ahead with the 11.00 am attack, even though it was now the early afternoon and the artillery preparation had long since ended. They made some piecemeal gains in the centre, and also on the left where elements of the *4e régiment* seized the ruins of the Château de la Motte. On the right, the *11e régiment* remained checked. Real progress on this wing depended on the valley on the regiment's flank being surrounded in conjunction with the *158e division* on the far side. Only then would it be possible to seize the carrières de Fruty that sat above the head of the valley. But the *158e division* failed to break the German defences facing it, and that in turn dashed any chance the *11e cuirassiers* had of gaining their objectives.

Brécard had already scaled back his ambitions for the day, intending to do no more than secure the edge of the plateau above Allemant. Even that proved beyond his grasp, for the resumption of the attack he had ordered for 6.00 pm never truly materialized. The *cuirassiers* were now too tired to mount a serious push, and in the evening they had to abandon the Château de la Motte.

Outcome

Towards dusk a thunderstorm turned the battlefield into a sea of mud, immobilizing the soldiers and filling the trenches and shell-holes with water. The attack had managed to break into the foremost position, but failed to generate enough tempo to break through it before the German reserves arrived to fill the gaps. Slow and unreliable communications left commanders out of touch with what was actually happening and prevented them from truly commanding.

The second day of the battle merely confirmed the outcome. A general attack was ordered to complete the conquest of the third intermediate objective, and was launched at 4.00 pm after a six-hour artillery preparation. 'I have just witnessed the assault waves of the *4e cuirassiers* setting off,' wrote a senior officer of the neighbouring division to the regiment's *colonel*. 'Your admirable soldiers, with their superb dash, filled me with enthusiasm.'

Yet their dash was in vain. The *cuirassiers* had no armoured support, since the ground had become so soaked that it was regarded as impracticable for tanks. On the right, the *11e régiment* gained just 200 metres. On the left, the *4e régiment* took the Château de la Motte, only to abandon it once more that evening in case the men occupying it

Ruins of the Château de la Motte.

were trapped by German counter-attacks. The advanced elements of the *9e régiment* also had to fall back from a quarry they had taken after descending into the head of the Allemant ravine.

An exaggerated victory

French propaganda inflated the capture of the moulin de Laffaux in an effort to boost morale. Yet it was no more than a partial success. The *cuirassiers* had lodged themselves into the German front at one of its most sensitive points, but had gained a depth of no more than 1.25 km of ground, which was not enough to make their position secure. The Germans had contained the attack on top of the plateau, and over the next five months repeatedly tried to win back the lost parts of the position. The moulin de Laffaux became a notorious point of friction. It has been compared to a thorn buried deep inside a wound and keeping it constantly inflamed. Difficult to capture, yet impossible to ignore, this formidable bastion continued to be contested until October, when the Germans finally abandoned the Chemin des Dames.

WHAT TO SEE

The tour starts at the moulin de Laffaux. You can easily reach this point from Soissons – just drive 10 km north-eastwards along the N2, until you come to the exit signposted for the D26. The moulin de Laffaux lies on the northern side of the N2, and has been turned into a rest area, where you will find toilets and a restaurant. We shall park here, at the centre of the battlefield, and then make excursions in various directions to visit key points. These excursions add up to a total distance of 20 km. You can drive much of the way if you wish, but you will need to walk to Points F, G and I, which are at the end of tracks. (To reach Point G by car, you would need to approach it from the east, from the Calvaire de l'Ange Gardien.)

Point A: Moulin de Laffaux

Note how this point dominates the surrounding area. At the time of the battle, the road junction lay immediately north of today's restaurant, but it became redundant when the N2 was displaced 120 metres southwards during its conversion into a dual carriageway. A cluster of French monuments has gradually accumulated at the original junction. Several of them were originally erected in the surrounding area, but

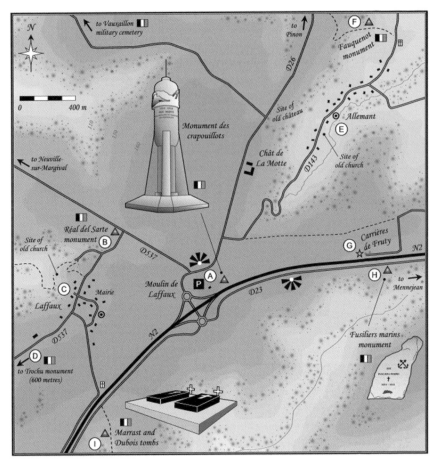

Tour III: Laffaux.

were moved here in the 1980s so they could be preserved more easily. The site underwent a major renovation in time for the centenary of the war, and the monuments now form a garden of remembrance.

Monument des crapouillots

The centrepiece of the garden is the massive *Monument des crapouillots.* Thirteen metres high, it honours the 12,000 men of the *artillerie de tranchée* – the trench mortars – who fell for France in the First World War. Trench mortars were close-range weapons ideal for providing instant fire support for the infantry or for devastating front-line trenches in preparation for an attack. (In contrast, 75mm field guns had too flat a trajectory, while the heavy artillery could not be used safely against targets so close to French lines.) Infantrymen might well grumble about trench mortars provoking German retaliation, yet they also drew reassurance from having such firepower immediately to hand instead of having to rely on a distant artillery battery.

Crapouillot was the nickname given to the trench mortarmen. It means 'little toad', and is a reference to the high-angled trajectory of a mortar round, similar to a toad's leap. The top of the monument shows a 58mm trench mortar being fired, and the shape of the monument itself is a simplified version of one of the winged bombs.

As well as remembering the fallen, the monument marks the passing of the *artillerie de tranchée* itself, for it was a short-lived arm. Improvised soon after the start of trench warfare, it outlived its usefulness once operations returned to the open country in 1918. The *crapouillots* distinguished themselves on many battlefields since their presence was so ubiquitous, and their monument might have been

Monument des crapouillots. The bas-relief shows a trench mortar being fired.

erected on any one of them. The main reason for the choice of Laffaux was that it lay more or less at the centre of the Western Front and within easy reach of Paris. The monument was inaugurated in September 1933. Twice it has undergone major restorations. Damaged by German shells in June 1940, it was repaired and re-inaugurated in 1958. In 2007 it was struck by lightning, and was then dismantled and rebuilt in its present location 150 metres further east.

Cuirassier memorials

Three monuments honour the *cuirassiers*. One of them has been dedicated by the *4e régiment* to all of Brécard's *cuirassiers*, while another is an individual memorial to *Maréchal des logis* Maurice Thiriez, who fell on 8 May. Of particular interest is the cross to the 5th Squadron of the *9e régiment*. So intense was the German machine-gun fire on the morning of 5 May that all the officers of the squadron fell soon after the start of the attack. First to be killed was the commander, *Capitaine comte* René de Chasteigner, a devout man strict on himself but indulgent to others. *Lieutenant* Michel Wagner took command, but was shot in the forehead on reaching the first German trench-line. His replacement, a Corsican called *Sous-lieutenant* Jean-Luc de Carbuccia, was mortally wounded shortly afterwards. 'Officer brimming with energy and courage' reads de Carbuccia's citation. 'Remarkable leader of men.' Then *Aspirant* Jean Parise was killed, so the most senior NCO, *Maréchal des logis* Jacques Domère, took command and led the remnants of the

Garden of remembrance at the moulin de Laffaux.

squadron to the assigned objective. After the battle, the survivors passed their fallen officers at a provisional cemetery behind the front. One of those present noted the men's eyes brimming with tears, and their jaws clenched with grief and the desire for revenge. 'I have never seen a more splendid march-past,' he recalled, 'an impeccable present-arms, a keeping-in-step that was amazing in this mud . . . It was something sublime.'

Other memorials

Among the other monuments is one to *Général de division* Eugène Estienne, the pragmatic visionary who helped create the French tank arm. Another was erected by the professional body representing stenographers, or shorthand writers, in memory of their fallen colleagues. At the entrance to the garden is a bunker dating from the Second World War. It has been turned into a memorial to the soldiers who fell in 1940, when fighting once again raged on the Chemin des Dames as the Germans unleashed a renewed onslaught into the heart of France following the Dunkirk evacuation.

Point B: Réal del Sarte monument

We shall now explore the surrounding area, starting with the western edge of the battlefield. Head north-westwards along the D537 for 575 metres until you come to a T-junction. The stone cross at the corner is a tribute to *Cavalier* Serge Réal del Sarte of the *9e cuirassiers*. He was mortally wounded near here on 30 April, shortly after his regiment had taken over the sector, and died at Soissons the next day (Stop 27). Serge's older brother, the sculptor Maxime, paid a special tribute to him when he designed the grandiose monument to the *Armées de Champagne* at Navarin, 37 km east of Reims. Three soldiers are shown on the top of that monument, each with the features of a specific individual, and the one charging with fixed bayonet represents Serge.

The cross to Serge Réal del Sarte.

Point C: Laffaux

From Réal del Sarte's monument, go along the road signposted for Laffaux. There is usually room to park in the *place Cholon*, the main village square outside the *mairie*. The village was already in ruins by the start of 1917. After the war it had to be rebuilt further east, on top of the plateau rather than on the upper slopes of the ravine, since some of the grottos and quarries beneath its previous location had collapsed. Only the western part of today's village overlaps with the original site. The reconstruction was financed in part by the town of Cholon in the French colony of Cochinchina. (Cholon is now a district of Ho Chi Minh City in southern Vietnam.)

Near the *mairie* stands the local war memorial, on which you will find a plaque to the *9e cuirassiers*. The Second World War bunker in front of the *mairie* was part of an entrenched camp that the Germans established in 1940 to the west of Laffaux where the railway line passes through a tunnel. Similar defensive works can be seen around the village.

The church has been rebuilt in a completely different location – its predecessor used to stand 400 metres to the north-west, on the slopes descending into the ravine. Inside are several plaques, including one listing the French regiments that served in this area during the war: 'Remember the brave men who suffered here and who in their fight for France's salvation made the moulin de Laffaux heartbreakingly yet gloriously famous all around the world.' Two other plaques commemorate the *Fusiliers marins*, who helped retake the moulin de Laffaux in September 1918. These two plaques were originally located outdoors, at sites that we shall visit later in this tour.

Point D: Trochu monument

From Laffaux, head south-westwards along the D537. After 1.1 km the road bends just before it enters the woods and descends into a valley. On the righthand side of the road at this bend is a monument to a 19-year-old French soldier, *Caporal* René Trochu of the *118e régiment*. He was killed by a shell on 7 April 1917, during an unsuccessful French attack ahead of the Nivelle offensive, and his body was never found.

Monument to Caporal Trochu.

Point E: Allemant

Return to the moulin de Laffaux. In our second excursion from this central point, we shall visit the Allemant valley in the northern-eastern corner of the battlefield. Head along the D26 in the direction of Pinon and then turn right on to the D143 (signposted for Allemant). The road winds its way down into the valley. German reserves were stationed near the base of these steep slopes, protected by them from the worst of the shelling. A couple of underground quarries served as depots and shelters. On the evening of 6 May, a dozen *cuirassiers* of the *9e régiment* broke into one of the quarries, led by an NCO called *Maréchal des logis* Rouziès. A firefight erupted in the dark interior and ended in the surrender of some fifty Germans, but Rouziès and his men then found themselves cut off by machine-gun fire and had to wait until nightfall before they could make their way back to the French lines 200 metres away. This was typical of the outcome whenever French detachments tried to push the attack beyond the edge of the plateau, since the terrain placed them at such a disadvantage. Once they ventured down the slopes, they were isolated and vulnerable to counter-attacks.

Continue along the D143 until you come to the south-western entrance of Allemant. To your right is the site of the old church, marked by a cross standing on a mound and surrounded by a few surviving stones. On the opposite side of the D143, 100 metres further on, you will see a road named the *Chemin de la Motte*. It used to lead up to the Château de la Motte at the top of the wooded slopes, but the *château* was completely destroyed during the war and has been rebuilt 500 metres nearer the moulin de Laffaux.

Elements of the *4e cuirassiers* conquered the ruined *château* on both 5 and 6 May, but were unable to hold it. The problem was that the *château* lay beyond the crest of the plateau, exposed to German counter-attacks but hidden from ground-based artillery observers watching the progress of the attack from the French rear. In the absence of reliable communications, the *cuirassiers* lacked effective artillery support and were even subjected to friendly fire.

Point F: Fauquenot monument

Continue through Allemant until you reach the local cemetery 175 metres beyond the village. At this point, a grass track branches off to the left. Walk up it and veer left when you come to the fork. Sixty metres further on is a monument to *Soldat* Jean Nicolas Fauquenot of the *49e régiment*, who was killed on 25 September 1918. His citation records that he remained at his post despite a heavy bombardment and refused to leave his comrades even though wounded. He was aged just 17.

Soldat Fauquenot.

Point G: Carrières de Fruty

It is best to retrace your steps to Allemant, since the track beyond Fauquenot's monument becomes overgrown. We shall now visit the carrières de Fruty on the eastern edge of the battlefield, and will do so on foot as part of the route lies along tracks. Follow the D143 back up to the plateau. When you reach the top and come to the point where the road bends sharply to the right to join the D26, turn left on to an unsignposted track leading eastwards across the fields. After following this track for 1.1 km, turn right at the corner of a fenced orchard. Continue round the perimeter of the orchard until you end up walking westwards alongside the N2. The carrières de Fruty lie hidden in the clump of trees 250 metres further on.

Known to the Germans as the *Reichskanzler-Höhle*, the quarries were used for storing food and ammunition and for sheltering reserves. Despite being heavily bombarded beforehand, they were one of the main obstacles that dislocated the attack. Note how they block the narrow strip of ground between the ravine to the south and the crest 300 metres to the north where the Germans had machine-gun nests. The right wing of the *11e cuirassiers* tried to reach the quarries, but found itself exposed to machine-gun fire from north, east and south. Tanks were unable to help, for the terrain prevented them from approaching.

French soldiers at the carrières de Fruty.

One of the entrances to the carrières de Fruty today.

You may have noticed a discoloration on the rocks above the quarry entrances. These are actually scorch-marks left by flamethrowers. On 14 September 1918, the area of the moulin de Laffaux fell to the French for a final time as the Allies advanced during the closing stages of the war. The carrières de Fruty were captured by the battalion of *Fusiliers marins*, which used flamethrowers and asphyxiating grenades to mop up the defenders. A monument to the *Fusiliers marins* stands on the other side of the N2, but to reach it we will have to return to the moulin de Laffaux.

Point H: *Fusiliers marins* monument
When you arrive back at the moulin de Laffaux, cross the bridge over the N2 to the roundabout on the southern side. Head north-eastwards along the D23, and you will reach the monument after 1.4 km. (Car parking is available on the opposite side of the road, should you decide to drive to this point.)

The *Fusiliers marins* have the dual role of guarding the navy's land-based installations and helping to protect its ships. At the start of the First World War, a brigade of them was created in order to use the navy's spare manpower as infantry. The brigade won fame defending the Belgian town of Dixmude in October–November 1914, thereby preventing the Germans from thrusting along the coast to Dunkirk and Calais. It was disbanded in November 1915, since by that stage the navy needed more men at sea, but a battalion remained on the Western Front until the end of the war. It was this battalion that took the carrières de Fruty in September 1918.

When inaugurated in 1938, the monument stood in front of the quarries, but had to be moved to its current location when the dual carriageway was built for the N2. Made from a block of Breton granite shaped like a menhir, it bears the insignia of the *Fusiliers marins*: a pair of crossed anchors.

Point I: Twin tombs of Marrast and Dubois

Return westwards along the D23. (If you are driving, you should park at the moulin de Laffaux and walk to this final point of the tour.) From the roundabout at the southern end of the bridge over the N2, continue along the D23 for another 950 metres as the road bends round to the south-west, and then take the unsignposted track on your left. It descends the southern slopes of the plateau, and on the right after 220 metres there is a small clump of trees, which shade a pair of tombs.

Lieutenant de vaisseau Pierre Marrast and *Enseigne de vaisseau* Jean Dubois were two officers of the *Fusiliers marins* who fell during the attack on 14 September 1918. The sheltered ground at this point was the location of their battalion's command post that morning, and it was here that their bodies were brought two nights later. They had served together in the same company for almost three years, and their families built twin tombs for them so they would remain united in death.

The direction in which the *Fusiliers marins* attacked was along the N2 towards the moulin de Laffaux. Marrast commanded the 3rd Company on the eastern side of the road. 'This longed-for day has come at last!' he exclaimed. Dubois had postponed his leave in order to take part. 'We are going to do something interesting here,' he wrote to his mother. 'Naturally, I will come only afterwards, for I will not leave my men.'

Dubois fell at the end of the attack, almost immediately after telling his orderly to pass him a firearm so he could shoot at a group of Germans. Shortly afterwards Marrast was also killed. 'Lads, we've reached our objective,' he told his men after arriving at the carrières de Fruty. Pulling out a map, he examined it with his monocle and confirmed: 'Yes, lads, I believe that's it. My hearty congratulations!' He began to dictate a report, and had just reached the point where Dubois had died when he himself was hit in the head by a bullet.

Some days earlier, Marrast had dismissed concerns that the *Fusiliers marins* battalion might be disbanded. 'That doesn't signify,' he said. 'We still have enough time to die with a flourish.'

Optional visits

You may wish to visit Mennejean farm (1.1 km south-east of Point H). The farm was in ruins by May 1917, but occupied a key point in front of the Chemin des Dames, blocking the top of a spur that protruded southwards towards Fort de Condé. At the crossroads 300 metres north-east of the farm you will find the grave of *Commandant* Marcel Demongeot, a battalion commander of the *230e régiment* who was mortally wounded during the German offensive in May 1918.

It is also worth visiting Montgarni farm (3.5 km west-south-west of the moulin de Laffaux), where a monument commemorates the fallen soldiers of the *13e division*. To reach the monument, stand outside the farm, walk 50 metres westwards along the D53, and take the track on the left immediately after you pass the Vuillery road. Six hundred French soldiers were provisionally buried at this point before being transferred to permanent cemeteries. One of them remains here: *Lieutenant* Guy Frémont, commander of a tank battery who died in the Laffaux sector during the Malmaison offensive on 23 October 1917. (The date is wrongly recorded on the monument.)

Tour IV
Craonne
4–6 May 1917

Of all the points of friction dotted along the Chemin des Dames, none became more notorious than the bastions at either end. We have already visited the moulin de Laffaux in the west, and we shall now explore its eastern counterpart, the plateau de Craonne.

From their observation points on the Craonne plateau, the Germans had superb views over the Aisne valley. Beginning at Hurtebise farm, the plateau juts out to the east of the Chemin des Dames to form an imposing, 4-km long promontory. Seen from above, it looks like a gnarled and crooked finger, since it repeatedly widens and contracts to create a string of three secondary plateaux – the triangular plateau de Vauclair, followed by the hunched plateau des Casemates, and finally the long, distorted rectangle of the plateau de Californie at the fingertip.

This tour focuses on the plateau de Californie. On the eve of the Nivelle offensive, it lay 1 km north of the French front line. Any attempt by the French to conquer the plateau would first have to seize the little town of Craonne perched immediately below its rim. The problem was that the slopes on either side of Craonne bulged outwards, creating two salients in the German front and exposing any direct assault on the shattered town to a deadly crossfire. By the start of May, the French had managed to gain only the western and southern parts of Craonne, and the plateau above remained firmly in German hands.

WHAT HAPPENED
The problem of Craonne was inherited by the *10e armée* when it was inserted in the front on 21 April. Its sector covered the 15-km arc from the eastern end of the Chemin des Dames to the Aisne. On its left wing, the *10e armée* planned a succession of two bite-and-hold attacks. The

18e corps would start by seizing the plateau de Craonne. A broader attack, including the adjacent *9e corps*, would then secure the right flank of the plateau by capturing the area at its eastern foot.

The *18e corps'* attack was eventually fixed for the morning of 5 May, and was coordinated with simultaneous onslaughts made by the *6e armée* further west along the Chemin des Dames. But in order to have a viable jumping-off line, the *18e corps* needed to obtain a foothold on the south-eastern tip of the plateau de Californie immediately above the town of Craonne. A preliminary attack was therefore planned for the evening of the 4th.

Craonne, 4–6 May 1917.

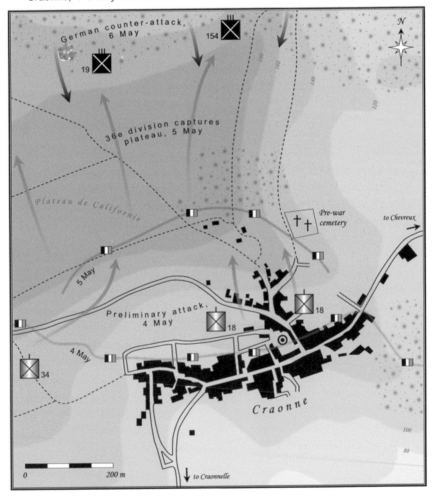

As well as relying on the firepower of the preparatory bombardment to devastate the German defences, the French sought a degree of tactical surprise. On the morning of the 4th, they made a feint attack by unleashing a rolling barrage on the whole front of the *18e corps*. The real attack came at 6.00 pm and was limited to the vicinity of Craonne. Two companies of the *18e régiment* attacked frontally while one from the *34e* assailed the German flank from the west. The terrain favoured this latter thrust, since on the western side of Craonne the French front line jutted outwards and enclosed a corner of high ground. For the Germans, this awkward angle in the front posed a double threat, as it not only dominated their trenches near Craonne, but also lay opposite the junction between the division responsible for holding the Craonne sector – the *28. Reserve-Infanterie-Division* – and its western neighbour.

Among those who watched the attack that evening was *Caporal* Georges Gaudy of the *35e division*. From his position 1 km further west, he saw black dots appear along the slope and deploy into extended order, forming two assault waves that rippled through the ocean of shell-holes:

> The first wave reached the edge of Craonne. At that moment it was hit by a 150mm shell, and dense curls of smoke rolled over the thin line as it scattered. Some Boche flares rose in desperate haste, and machine-gun fire could be heard in fits and starts. The black figures dispersed and were swallowed up in the cavities of the ground, before appearing again and regrouping. They entered the ruins, mounting the heaps of rubble and passing through the smashed walls.

The leading wave reached the rim of the plateau. For a moment, the men were silhouetted against the sky, but then abruptly disappeared into shellholes and began to consolidate the conquered position. By 6.35 pm all three assault companies had gained their objectives. Losses were light, for the artillery preparation had been effective and the Germans unleashed their own barrage too late.

Nor did the attackers have to face a powerful counter-thrust. The unit holding the plateau de Californie, *Reserve-Infanterie-Regiment Nr 111*, had suffered a disaster before the attack even began. Unable to

Craonne early in the war.

A group of French soldiers next to the ruins of Craonne in 1917.

A street in Craonne in 1917.

distribute its reserves behind the front owing to a lack of bombproof shelters, it had to concentrate two companies inside a 260-metre long tunnel. That morning, a French shell scored a direct hit on the main entrance, blowing up a stockpile of ammunition and trapping the men inside. The regimental commander gave the order to escape through an emergency exit lest the men suffocate in the smoke and fumes. But a young officer, unaware of this order, persuaded the men to move back into the rear part of the tunnel and build a sandbag barricade to contain the smoke. They then tried to pierce a shaft through the roof, but found it so difficult to breathe that they had to abandon the attempt. As despair grew, some men shot themselves or slit their wrists.

Rescue attempts could achieve little in the absence of specialist breathing equipment. A party of combat engineers entered the tunnel in the evening to try to reach any survivors, but as their leader explained, it was hopeless:

> After a few steps the light already grew dim, and in the end it failed completely. We were already gasping for breath, and the acrid smoke caused constant coughing. Sweat ran from every

pore. We then stumbled over some bodies. They were taken outside and we continued onwards very slowly, but when we tried shouting we received no reply. Dead silence, except for the roar and crash of shells outside.

A mere handful of men escaped from the tunnel, and the disaster left the regiment without a reserve. Despite requesting reinforcements, it received none before the French attacked Craonne that evening. Only towards dawn on the 5th did a battalion arrive from another unit of the *28. Reserve-Infanterie-Division*, and by then the moment had long passed for making a surprise counter-thrust while the situation was still fluid.

Main attack

A heavy bombardment on the morning of the 5th heralded a further French onslaught. The capture of Craonne was a mere curtain-raiser for the main attack that was now about to be unleashed on a far larger scale. Two divisions of the *18e corps* waited side-by-side on a front extending from Craonne more than 3.5 km westwards to the vicinity of Hurtebise farm. On the right, the *36e division* prepared to pounce on the plateau de Californie, while the *35e division* had the task of taking the adjoining plateaux on the left. *Caporal* Gaudy was waiting to go over the top:

> Time passed. You longed for the day to break, and yet you also feared the day. It crossed my mind that I might die that morning. If I fell at the start of the attack, I would be cold and stiff by the time the sun set that evening. How would I be killed – by a shell-splinter or by a bullet? I would prefer a bullet, in either my forehead or my heart.

The objective of the *36e division* was to gain the northern and eastern edges of the plateau de Californie. From there, it would be able to see into the Ailette valley and call down barrages to shatter any German preparations to recapture the plateau. At 9.00 am the division opened its attack, with four battalions in the first line. Sticking closely to the rolling barrage, three of them reached the edge of the plateau in a single bound within fifteen minutes. The fourth was temporarily checked by machine-gun fire and took ten minutes longer. As on the previous evening, resistance was light and losses minimal. So demoralized were many of the Germans after enduring the endless drumfire that they welcomed captivity as their only chance of survival.

The French began to consolidate the captured position. They organized three successive lines of defence, dug communication trenches from the rear, and brought up supplies. Yet holding the plateau proved more difficult and costly than capturing it. The tableland protruded northwards, leaving it exposed to German artillery fire from both front and flank. By 11.00 am the bombardment had become so concentrated that the French engineers found it almost impossible to continue fortifying the position. The *36e division* was reinforced in the afternoon with the *218e régiment* from the corps reserve. Already the division was becoming ground down by the relentless shelling – so much so that it had to relieve one of its battalions from the front line that night.

German response

The French bite-and-hold attacks proved an effective answer to the German system of defence-in-depth. The limited objectives on 5 May were a sharp contrast to the unrealistic ambitions of 16 April. Seizing the plateau de Californie had required a forward bound of barely 500 metres, and this not only ensured that the preliminary bombardment could devastate all the entrenchments that had to be taken, but also allowed the infantry to reorganize after the attack and dig in before the German reserves had time to arrive.

The *28. Reserve-Infanterie-Division* did eventually manage to launch a counter-thrust in the afternoon of the 5th. But this riposte, by two battalions brought forward from the rear, was hurriedly prepared and lacked proper artillery support. Hindered by the marshy forest, it fell apart under heavy fire and came to a standstill near the foot of the northern slopes.

Only by committing a fresh division could the Germans hope to regain the plateau. An *Eingreif* unit, the *9. Infanterie-Division*, was belatedly released in the evening of the 5th, and a powerful counter-attack was arranged for the following morning. Six battalions from three regiments – *Infanterie-Regimente Nr 56, Nr 19* and *Nr 154* – were to carry out the assault. (Two of them came from the *9. Infanterie-Division*, and the third from a neighbouring *Eingreif-Division*.) Since the attack had no chance of taking the French by surprise, it depended on a thorough artillery preparation. For four hours the Germans kept up the bombardment. 'The heights were under intense fire,' recalled a soldier of *Infanterie-Regiment Nr 154*:

> We could hear thousands of shells of every calibre bursting up there, but without being able to distinguish the individual explosions. It was just a continuous rumble and thunder. Clouds of smoke shrouded the hilltop.

The dust and smoke made it difficult for French units to communicate to either flank, yet in terms of destruction the shelling proved less effective than the Germans hoped. At 8.47 am on the 6th they began the attack. A company commander of *Infanterie-Regiment Nr 19* saw friendly aircraft whizzing overhead:

> Fired up by their incredible bravery, we bounded from shellhole to shellhole. Now the enemy barrage set in: immense, black sprays from the explosions sprang up in front and behind us, trying to prevent us from passing. Shell splinters and clumps of earth whistled through the air, while tree-stumps disintegrated. We were right in the thick of the barrage.

Infanterie-Regiment Nr 19 lost 60 per cent of its men that day, and a staggering 80 per cent of its officers. The disparity is explained largely by the insistence of the battalion and company commanders on personally leading the assault. One of the subalterns could see the plateau in front of him, wrapped in dense smoke from the artillery bombardment. 'We passed through the barrage with incomparable courage,' he recalled, 'but no one had time to worry about the others. If anyone fell, he fell.'

Within half-an-hour the attack had gained the northern edge of the heights. But thereafter progress was patchy. In the east, for example, *Infanterie-Regiment Nr 154* was contained near the rim of the plateau by a combination of counter-attacks and artillery fire. Only in the centre did the situation become critical for the French. The *34e régiment* fell back to the middle of the plateau, and its support battalion was crushed by the bombardment. For a while the regiment was in danger of disintegrating to leave a gap through which the Germans might push, but the threat was averted in the afternoon when a battalion from the divisional reserve intervened in order to relieve the *34e* and regain the lost ground.

So intense was the shelling that part of the plateau was unoccupied by either side for much of the day. The German infantry remained on the northern edge, reluctant to incur excessive losses by venturing on to the exposed tabletop. Not until the evening was the empty ground reoccupied by a company of the French *218e régiment*.

As the battle petered out, units on both sides were relieved. A German soldier described how he felt when he marched to the rear. It was the month of May, and the countryside behind the lines was green and full of life:

> Behind us lay the smashed trenches of the [plateau de Californie]. Our minds were numb and weary, and wrestled with grief for those we had to leave behind. . . . Again and again the terrible memories came back to us. Yet our will to live began to stir, and the further we went, the lighter grew our steps and the freer our hearts. By the time the moon rose and we mounted our horses to ride to our rest quarters, May had triumphed in us and we were restored to life.

July 1917: the commander of the 18e corps decorates the flags of the three infantry regiments of the 36e division.

For the French, the capture of the plateau de Californie was an incomplete success. Their position was precarious, since the Germans were lodged on the northern slopes and could make sudden assaults whenever they chose. Nor did the French manage to accomplish the essential second stage of their plan. The seizure of the plateau was meant to be followed by an attack in the plain further east near Chevreux, but when the attack was launched on 8 May it gained little more than the first German trench. This failure left the plateau de Californie exposed on its flank and ensured that it remained permanently insecure.

WHAT TO SEE

Almost the whole of this tour is confined to tracks and has to be done on foot. The total walking distance is 5 km. Either before or after the tour, you may wish to visit the *Monument des Basques* (Stop 14). This is the memorial to the *36e division*, and stands just over 2 km to the south-west on the plateau de Vauclair.

Point A: Site of Craonne

Craonne was completely wiped out. The ground where it once stood has been turned into a tree garden, or arboretum, which you are free to explore on foot. (You will find a car park at the northern entrance, at the side of the D18 CD.) Amidst the trees and the distinct pock-marks left by the shelling, a few lingering traces of the town are still visible, including some of the paving-stones.

After the First Battle of the Aisne in 1914, the German front line stabilized along the southern edge of Craonne. Many houses had been badly damaged, but others were still reasonably intact. The church, which stood in the highest part of the town, had lost its steeple to German artillery fire on 14 September, owing to the suspected presence of French machine-guns in the tower.

Craonne was destroyed two-and-a-half years later at the time of the Nivelle offensive. Shells smashed the cellars of the houses, which were being used as shelters by the Bavarian soldiers holding this sector. The town's water supply was also wrecked and flooded the nearby shellholes. *Caporal* Georges Gaudy watched from afar as the French artillery pummelled the ruins again on 4 May 1917:

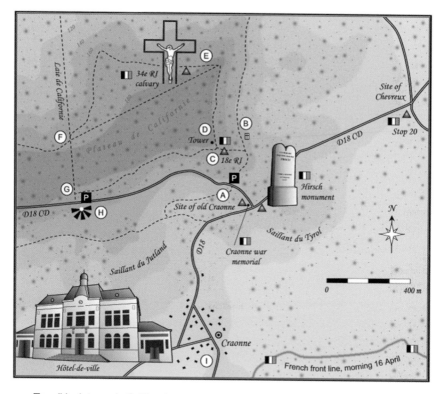

Tour IV: plateau de Californie.

Craonne tottered once more, disintegrated, and collapsed in fragments. You had the impression of power-hammers repeatedly striking, pulverizing, crushing. When the smoke momentarily dispersed, the last remnant of the [church] vault appeared, supported by its two pillars, still standing amidst the general chaos.

From the car park, the D18 CD descends 125 metres to a T-junction. Here, in the heart of the destroyed town, stands Craonne's war memorial. Two of the three faces list some of the French soldiers who fell in the surrounding area – a small selection of names representing thousands of others. On the third face are recorded the town's own fallen sons, including 23-year-old *Caporal* Julien Dhordain. By a quirk of

Ruins of Craonne church in 1917.

Site of Craonne church today.

fate, he was killed just 15 km away at Soupir on 16 April 1917 while serving in the *25e bataillon de chasseurs à pied*.

At the roadside 40 metres further east is a monument to a French Jewish officer, *Lieutenant* Joseph-Adolphe Hirsch. 'Outstanding officer, whose zeal and bravery were beyond all praise' reads his citation. Hirsch commanded a *section* of engineers in Company 18/52 of the *2e régiment du génie*. His *section* was entrenching the conquered plateau de Californie on the morning of 5 May 1917 when he was severely wounded by a shell. He died two-and-a-half hours later at a first-aid post at Craonne.

Point B: Craonne cemetery
We shall now explore the plateau de Californie. Return to the car park and take the track at its eastern end, signposted for Yves Gibeau. Follow the track for 200 metres as it curves round the tip of the plateau. Ignore the turning to the left signposted for the *tour observatoire*, and continue for another 50 metres, following the sign for Saint-Victor, until you see some tombs amid the trees on your right. This is the old cemetery of Craonne. Among the graves is that of French novelist Yves Gibeau, who died in 1994. He lived just 8 km from the Chemin des Dames, and was buried here in accordance with his wish:

> Something irresistible draws me back to this little path in old Craonne. So many times. So many hours spent watching the wild grasses stirring on the tombs, and listening to the rustle of the tall fir and all the nearby trees.

From the cemetery, return the same way until you reach the turning signposted for the *tour observatoire*. Walk 150 metres up this track to the concrete blockhouse near the top.

Point C: Memorial to the *18e régiment*
The blockhouse marks the south-eastern tip of the plateau de Californie. This point was taken by the *18e régiment* on the evening of 4 May, despite the steepness of the slopes. The regiment had a proud history. 'Brave *18e*, I know you,' Napoleon had declared. 'The enemy won't stand in front of you.' A memorial has been added to the top of the blockhouse. The citation inscribed on the plaque reads: 'Elite

Memorial to the 18e régiment.

regiment, entrusted with seizing the plateau de Craonne – a position reckoned to be impregnable – took it by assault in a superb dash.'

But the regiment's glory came at too high a price. Between 4 and 8 May, the *36e division* lost more than 2,500 officers and men killed, wounded or missing. High casualties necessitate a high turnover of divisions. Yet more frequent reliefs also mean shorter rest periods, which sometimes have to be abruptly curtailed. It was one of these sudden recalls to the front that sparked a mutiny in the *18e* just three weeks after it had distinguished itself at Craonne. (See Stop 35.)

Point D: Observation tower
From the blockhouse, walk up to the nearby observation tower. Inaugurated in 2013, it is 20 metres tall and commands sweeping views to the south and east. After dark, a blue light shines at the top in memory of the fallen. Ironically, this superb vantage point allows you to

see little of the plateau de Californie itself, which is now covered in forest. The trees have completely changed its appearance. Before 1914, only the lower slopes were wooded, for the tabletop was farmland. The wartime bombardments blasted away fields and trees alike, leaving the plateau completely denuded. From afar it seemed to be covered in snow, since the dazzling white limestone beneath the soil was exposed by the shelling.

After the war, the devastated regions were divided into coloured zones according to their degree of damage. The red zone was the worst affected and was deemed too badly ravaged to be worth recovering as farmland. Yet the extent of this zone was gradually reduced as a result of popular pressure, and most of the Chemin des Dames was eventually cleared and brought back into cultivation. Only the plateau de Californie and the adjacent plateau des Casemates have never been recovered – they were instead acquired by the State and turned into a forest.

The name *Californie* came from a park on the eastern edge of the plateau with a US-style saloon and a garden with exotic plants. Before the war, it was a place for an afternoon excursion, somewhere to relax and enjoy the views. The German name for the plateau was the *Winterberg*, for it reminded soldiers from the Sauerland region of a similar height they knew at home.

Point E: Calvary of the *34e régiment*

Follow the track that leads past the eastern foot of the tower and into the forest. After 350 metres, the track reaches the north-eastern corner of the plateau and bends round to the left. Immediately afterwards, you come to a fork. Ignore the track that branches off to the left – it cuts diagonally through the forest – and instead take the track on the right along the northern edge of the plateau. After 150 metres, you will see a calvary amidst the undergrowth on the southern side of the path. Dedicated to the fallen of the *34e régiment*, it remembers two men in particular: *Lieutenant* André Lafont and *Sergent* Rémi Leveau, who were killed on 6 May. Both their names are recorded on the Craonne war memorial (Point A).

Points F and G: Remains of trenches

One of the beneficial side-effects of the forestation of the plateau is that

Lunar landscape: the pockmarked summit of the plateau de Californie.

it has preserved traces of the trenches and shellholes. Elsewhere on the Chemin des Dames, they were mostly filled in when local inhabitants reclaimed the ground and turned it back into farmland, but on this tour you can still see remnants at various points.

Follow the track along the northern and north-western edges of the plateau. When you reach the *retour parking* sign, the track veers round to the left and heads south along a firebreak in the forest called the *Laie de Californie*. Slightly further on, a diagonal track crosses the firebreak and the remnants of some trenches can be found immediately west of this point. Traces of others survive 200 metres further south, on the western side of the firebreak just before it reaches the D18 CD.

Point H: Viewpoint

Cross to the far side of the D18 CD, where you will find an orientation table and views extending over the Aisne valley. To the north of the road is the site of one of the most controversial memorials on the Chemin des Dames – a sculpture by Haïm Kern that was stolen in August 2014. Entitled *ils n'ont pas choisi leur sépulture* ('they had no choice of tomb'), it was almost 4 metres high and depicted human heads trapped in a bronze mesh. Its inauguration in November 1998 by Lionel Jospin, the Socialist prime minister, sparked a bitter political dispute, for Jospin's speech called for the shame associated with the mutinies of 1917 to give way to understanding, and for executed French soldiers to be restored in the collective memory of the nation.

Craonne has become inextricably bound up with the mutinies because its name was immortalized in a popular anti-war song, the *Chanson de Craonne*. Yet the song went through several adaptations and was associated with Craonne only after being linked with several other battlefields. Far from seeing any concentration of disorders, Craonne was actually the scene on 4 May 1917 of one of the most successful and well-planned French attacks on the Chemin des Dames. The mutinies themselves have been misinterpreted, and are often appropriated today by pacifists. The measures taken to suppress the indiscipline were actually a mixture of repression and conciliation, and only 3 per cent of the men punished for taking part in the most serious disorders were shot.

From the northern side of the D18 CD, head eastwards along the track above the car park, following the signposts for the *départ micro balade* and the *tour observatoire*. When you reach the observation tower, return to Point A and collect your car. To end the tour, we shall drive to the rebuilt town of Craonne, which lies 1 km to the south-west along the D18.

Point I: Craonne

Several towns or villages in the Chemin des Dames area were never rebuilt. Others, including Craonne, were rebuilt in a different location, either because it was easier to do so on ground unencumbered by ruins, or because the new site offered more advantages than the old. Craonne is now 40 metres less elevated than before, and is more protected by the plateau from cold north winds. Rebuilding the town took a decade, and the place never really recovered. Even in the 1930s its population was less than one-third of the pre-war figure, and has now shrunk to a mere one-eighth.

One of the oddities of Craonne is the size of the *hôtel-de-ville*, which is ridiculously large for a town of fewer than eighty inhabitants. It is actually a gift from Sweden, which helped finance the town's reconstruction. Despite Sweden's neutrality during the war, some of its citizens fought on the French side, and a plaque on the staircase landing explains that the *hôtel-de-ville* is a memorial to those of them who were killed near Craonne.

Tour V
The Malmaison Offensive
23 October 1917

At the start of November 1917, six months after Nivelle's first colossal onslaught, the Germans finally abandoned their remaining positions on the Chemin des Dames. This tour examines the decisive defeat that compelled them to withdraw – their loss of the western end of the plateau to the Malmaison offensive launched on 23 October. We shall focus on one specific and vital part of the line: the area around Fort de la Malmaison, the dominant point of high ground that gave its name to the offensive as a whole.

WHAT HAPPENED

The offensive was long in preparation. The initial concept began to take shape in May, but it was repeatedly postponed owing to concerns about the French army's morale and pressing priorities elsewhere on the Western Front. Not until 15 September was the plan finalized.

Every aspect of the operation was weighted to favour the attackers, for an army still brittle from a nervous breakdown could not risk a setback. *Général de division* Paul Maistre, the commander of the *6e armée*, wrote:

> The Chemin des Dames has a bad reputation, in the interior of the country as much as amongst the troops. Another failed operation in this region would have a disastrous effect. At all costs, we must be certain of success, and the first condition of this certainty is a crushing superiority in artillery.

The attack zone was just 11 km wide, and shallow enough to be thoroughly pounded by the preliminary bombardment. In effect, the artillery would carry out the attack, and the infantry would then occupy the ground conquered by the shelling. In contrast to the over-ambitious

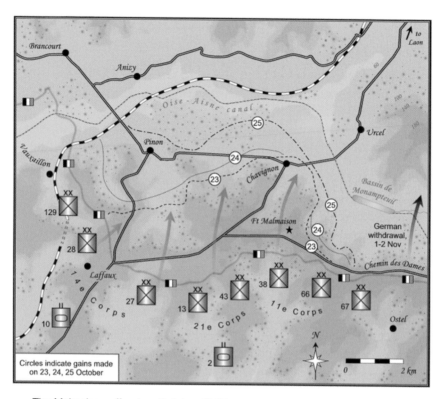

The Malmaison offensive, October 1917.

offensive of 16 April, objectives were limited and realistic. There was no question of trying to break right through the German fortified zone, for a deep thrust, far from closing down the interminable agony of the Chemin des Dames, would merely have prolonged it by creating a useless and over-extended salient. The French simply sought to gain the crucial high ground at the western end of the Chemin des Dames. Since this end of the plateau jutted northwards, its conquest would make the whole German position on the Chemin des Dames untenable by enabling French artillery observers to see behind it along the curve of the Ailette valley.

German dilemma
By September, the Germans realized the likelihood of a big attack in this area. It is clear with hindsight that they should have evaded the

blow and withdrawn while they still could, but after expending so much blood to hold the Chemin des Dames they could not tamely abandon it without handing the French a propaganda triumph. Some senior German officers believed that the plateau could be held, and still thought in terms of using it to launch an offensive of their own at some stage in the future.

The only realistic way of holding this part of the Chemin des Dames was a forward defence, since the terrain and the weight of French firepower would prevent the swift movement of reserves. Large numbers of troops had to be placed in, or immediately behind, the *I Stellung*, even though this exposed them to the brunt of the bombardment. The French deliberately chose to attack the area near Laffaux, where the German front was bent back to form an exposed corner. The Germans were all the more vulnerable here because the units holding the front were isolated by the Oise–Aisne canal running along the marshy and gas-filled Ailette valley in their rear. To complicate matters even further, the valley formed a great, northward loop, which meant that German field guns sited behind the canal would be too distant to support the front-line units. Instead, many of the German batteries had to be placed south of the canal, where they were overcrowded and difficult to resupply.

The Germans recognized the critical importance of the area around Fort de la Malmaison. The fort itself was obsolete, but commanded views in all directions and blocked access to a long spur protruding into the Ailette valley. The élite *2. Garde-Infanterie-Division* was inserted to hold this part of the front, and could do so in strength since its sector was just 2.5 km wide. Two of its infantry regiments (*Garde-Grenadier-Regimente Nr 2* and *Nr 4*) occupied the *I Stellung*. The third regiment (*Garde-Grenadier-Regiment Nr 1*) was in reserve, but distributed the companies of one of its battalions in close support of the *I Stellung*.

The neighbouring German divisions held fronts that were up to 1 km wider. They had to place all three of their infantry regiments in the line, and were left with no units in close support. Hence detachments from the *Eingreif-Divisionen* had to be drawn forward and placed right behind the *I Stellung*. Unavoidable though this was, it resulted in some of the detachments suffering so heavily from the bombardment that they had to be relieved even before the start of the French attack.

Furthermore, the rumps of the *Eingreif-Divisionen* were too depleted to make powerful counter-thrusts, and so the German commanders lost much of their ability to influence the impending battle.

Massed firepower

The bombardment began on the evening of 16 October, and was overwhelming in its intensity. Three years into the war, the French army was finally overcoming its worst handicap of 1914 – its dire shortage of modern heavy artillery. La Malmaison was an extreme example of the massive concentrations of firepower that had been the dominant feature of attacks on the Western Front since 1915. The French enjoyed air superiority, which made observation easier than in April, and were able to direct fire inwards against the curved German position from either flank. Yet even at La Malmaison the early signs could be seen of the decisive shift in artillery tactics that occurred towards the end of 1917. The emphasis was starting to turn towards neutralization – the attempt not to destroy a defensive system but to incapacitate its defenders long enough for an attack to succeed. The plentiful use of gas shells, for example, caused few actual fatalities but exhausted the German soldiers by forcing them to wear their uncomfortable gasmasks all day. Machine-guns were massed close behind the French first lines and directed an overhead, plunging fire against key points in the German rear such as crossroads, bridges and command posts. By interdicting German movements, the bombardment almost cut off the infantrymen holding the *I Stellung*, leaving them short of drinking water and deprived of hot food and regular reliefs. An artillery liaison officer with the *13. Infanterie-Division* wrote:

> The conditions in front were very disturbing, and the men were demoralized . . . The general view was that the attack would come in the next day or so. We knew it would be a fight against the odds owing to our immense losses and the great superiority clearly enjoyed by the enemy, and yet we sensed that everyone would welcome it as a release from this unbearable uncertainty.

The artillery preparation was meant to last just four days, since the sheer amount of firepower available shortened the time needed to produce results. It was extended to six days only because of adverse weather.

This brevity was another feature of future offensives. In the coming months, innovative techniques would slash the duration of bombardments even further, and make it possible to restore surprise to the battlefield with sudden and accurate concentrations of fire compressed into a matter of hours.

Assault division

Three army corps were assembled to carry out the attack, with a total of six divisions in the first line and six in support. Two additional divisions protected the flanks. The main thrust was entrusted to the three divisions in the centre – the *38e division* and the neighbouring *21e corps* – which were favoured with a higher concentration of artillery support and a disproportionate number of tank batteries.

The *38e division* had an outstanding reputation and was frequently used to spearhead assaults. Its front line lay some 600 metres south of the Chemin des Dames roadway. On the far side of the road, a spur

Attack by the 38e division, 23 October 1917.

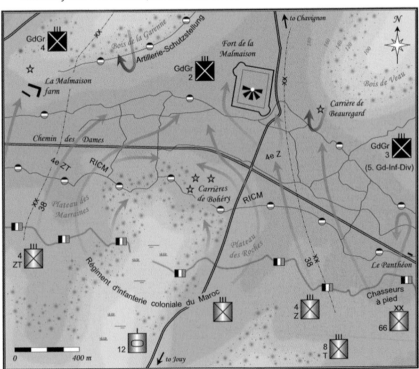

Attack zone of the 38e division, seen from the air.

jutted north-eastwards into the Ailette valley, and on the highest point of that spur, where it began to protrude from the plateau, sat Fort de la Malmaison. The division had to conquer the fort and then descend the far end of the spur to the foot of the valley. It would carry out this advance of some 3.5 km in two stages. The first objective lay 1.4 km away, and encompassed both the fort and the whole of the *I Stellung*.

The terrain ruled out a straightforward, frontal attack. The division had a front of 1.5 km, but had to jump off from either side of an unassailable ravine, leaving an 800-metre gap in its centre. The ravine could not be ignored, for at its head the Germans had established a labyrinth of strongpoints in the carrières de Bohéry. The *Régiment d'infanterie coloniale du Maroc (RICM)*, which straddled the ravine, had to eliminate the threat posed by these quarries as the division advanced beyond them. The solution was bold and imaginative: the regiment was split into two wings, which would sweep round either side of the *carrières*, link up on the Chemin des Dames to the north, and then mop up the encircled strongholds.

Zero hour

Despite the obvious imminence of the offensive, the French commanders could still achieve an element of tactical surprise if they chose the right moment to attack. Zero hour was initially fixed for 5.45 am on the 23rd, but the Germans found this out while interrogating prisoners and planned to unleash a bombardment shortly beforehand so as to catch the assault troops waiting in their crowded trenches. However, the French were alerted by an intercepted radio message. Realizing that the attack time had been compromised, they brought it forward to 5.15 am, even though this was an hour before sunrise.

When the attack began, the spearhead battalions had to use compasses to carry out their complex manoeuvres in the dark. Even as the sky lightened, the entire area remained shrouded by mist and gas, but the poor visibility hindered both sides. The defenders were unable to recover and bring their machine-guns into action before the French infantry reached the first trench close behind the rolling barrage. Entire German companies were captured when assailed from the flank or rear after the adjacent positions were broken through. Many of the close-support units were overrun before they could react, and even those that did manage to launch a counter-thrust were soon pinned down.

Fort de la Malmaison from the air.

In less than an hour, the *38e division* had gained its first objective. The two prongs of the *RICM* had linked up as planned north of the carrières de Bohéry, and the *4e zouaves* had seized Fort de la Malmaison. The only major hitch so far was the loss of the entire *groupe* of twelve fighting tanks that had been assigned to support the division. This *groupe, AS12,* was split into two halves so it could operate on either side of the ravine of the carrières de Bohéry. Yet only the eastern half actually managed to reach the front line and join the attack, and every one of those tanks either ditched or broke down in the soaked and cratered ground, or was knocked out by artillery fire. It was a powerful argument against producing limited numbers of mechanically fragile behemoths. Their flaws, starkly exposed in three successive engagements on the Aisne in 1917, encouraged a switch in emphasis to a smaller, lighter and faster tank, the Renault FT17, which could be mass-produced.

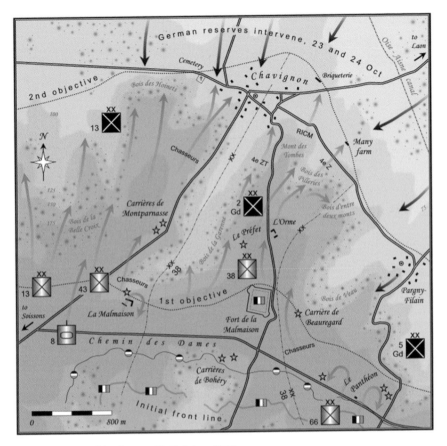

Phase two: Chavignon, 23 October 1917.

Renewed advance

The attack paused after reaching the first objective. The rationale for building this interval into the schedule was to compensate for any delays and ensure that progress remained properly coordinated. It was important to avoid the problems that had occurred in previous attacks, when the rolling barrage had outpaced the infantry by sticking to an over-ambitious timetable, or when attempts to resume a stalled advance by improvising a new plan had foundered on the problems of communication. The pause enabled the second phase to be preceded by a methodical bombardment and spearheaded by a new set of three battalions that moved forward from the rear. The drawback was that these battalions had to endure a wait of around three hours, since the advance was due to resume only at 9.15 am. Men who had begun the day keyed up found their nervous tension ebbing away, making it hard for them to advance when the time finally came.

The second phase of the attack proved more costly than the first. The *38e division* struggled to progress along the exposed spur beyond Fort de la Malmaison. The ground was swept by machine-gun fire from either flank, for the neighbouring divisions had run into tough resistance and had been unable to keep pace. Nor were any of the tanks of *AS12* left to support the infantry. Of the three battalions in the *RICM*, the one that spearheaded the second phase suffered 42 per cent of the regiment's total losses that day. Thirteen of that battalion's seventeen officers were out of action, and their loss was particularly grievous since men without leaders were liable to take cover instead of moving forward.

The far end of the spur splits into three rounded stubs separated by the wooded ravines of the Bois des Pilleries and the Bois d'entre deux monts. The officers in charge of a couple of the spearhead battalions used their initiative to exploit what cover was available. The battalion of the *4e zouaves*, for example, ignored a planned 20-minute pause in the advance and boldly passed through its own artillery barrage rather than wait on top of the exposed terrain. It also inclined to the left into the neighbouring regiment's sector in order to be more sheltered from the machine-gun fire coming from its right flank.

Chasseurs advancing in single-file columns on the eastern flank of the 38e division. In the background on the left is the shapeless mass of Fort de la Malmaison.

Once the units descended into the Ailette valley, they suffered fewer casualties. By 11.45 am, the *38e division* had gained its second and final objective for the day – a line running around the northern side of Chavignon village and then south-eastwards along the foot of the heights. By pushing its advanced elements into the valley, it could prevent the Germans from launching counter-attacks from ground close to the base of the slopes, out of sight from the top of the plateau.

Aftermath

The German response was confused and fragmentary. Senior officers lacked enough information about what was happening in front. The *Eingreif-Divisionen* immediately behind the Malmaison sector had already been weakened before the attack, and some of their elements went astray or were delayed by artillery fire as they moved forward in response to the French onslaught. Too many parts of different units ended up in the same area – the reserves of the *2. Garde-Infanterie-Division* and assorted units from two *Eingreif-Divisionen* – and it proved impossible to coordinate them into a powerful and synchronized onslaught.

Some German counter-attacks did belatedly materialize during the afternoon of the 23rd, but lacked the advantage of surprise and were simply too weak. Their only significant achievement was to drive the French temporarily from the north-western part of Chavignon. Nor did it prove possible to launch a general counter-attack on the 24th. Any such attack would have been hopeless because the French controlled the dominating heights and could bring too much firepower to bear, whereas the Germans had lost much of their own artillery and lacked the means for an intense preliminary bombardment.

On the 25th, after a day's pause, the French mounted another push, and by the end of the 26th occupied the entire south bank of the Oise–Aisne canal. The German high command had already resigned itself to abandoning the whole length of the Chemin des Dames, and completed the final stage of this withdrawal in the night of 1/2 November.

Methodical planning and the sheer scale of resources devoted to the offensive had made the outcome almost a foregone conclusion. Yet France could not afford such a vast expenditure of ammunition for every attack, nor muster such superior resources for a larger operation on a wide front. No bombardment, however massive, could be expected to blot out an entire defensive system, and an excessive reliance on artillery risked undermining the infantrymen's own offensive power by sapping their flexibility and determination. Even at La Malmaison, bold leadership and improvisation had been required from the infantry despite the intensity of the preliminary bombardment. The *38e division* had demonstrated these qualities, but it was an experienced attack formation, and few units could match the quality of its officers or the prestige and self-confidence of its regiments. La Malmaison was one answer to the deadlock of trench warfare, but it was not the ultimate solution.

WHAT TO SEE
Point A: Aizy-Jouy
The tour is 11 km long. Most of it can be driven, but we shall park at various stages along the route to explore the vicinity on foot. Start at Aizy-Jouy, 14 km north-east of Soissons. This area was held by the Germans until Nivelle's attacks in April 1917 forced them to pull back to the crest of the Chemin des Dames. On the eve of the Malmaison offensive, the twin villages of Aizy and Jouy lay 1.5 km behind the French front line.

Follow the main street through the two villages. Inside Jouy, it bends left to pass round the church, but you should turn off it here and take the minor, unsignposted road that continues straight ahead to the north. The road climbs up to the plateau des Roches, which was the jumping-off point for the eastern wing of the *38e division*.

Point B: Plateau des Roches
After emerging from the woods, continue 200 metres along the top of the open plateau and then pause at the roadside. To your left is the marshy and wooded ravine that posed such problems during the planning of the attack. It was dominated by the quarries at its head, which the Germans had turned into an advanced bastion covering Fort de la Malmaison. These quarries had to be encircled by the two prongs of the *RICM*, and then mopped up with the help of tear-gas grenades.

Point C: *Lieutenant* d'Arnoux
Go another 300 metres northwards. You are now in what used to be no

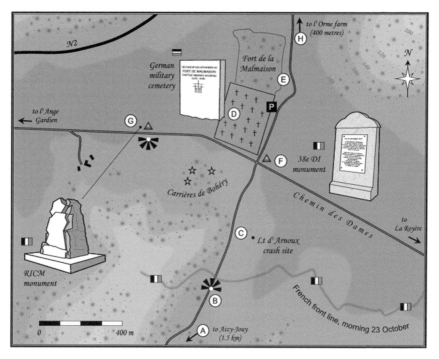

Tour V: Fort de la Malmaison.

man's land during the weeks before the Malmaison offensive. The fields 100 metres to the east of this point were the scene of a remarkable tale of survival against the odds. The central figure of the story was a 21-year-old French aviator called *Lieutenant* Jacques d'Arnoux. Early in the morning of 6 September 1917, he was flying as an observer in a two-seater Sopwith when it was pounced on by a couple of German aircraft in the skies above Fort de la Malmaison. The pilot was shot dead and the Sopwith plunged earthwards – until for some unknown reason it suddenly pulled up and skimmed 300 metres over the trenches. *Lieutenant* d'Arnoux then passed out. On coming to, he found he was lying on his back within 100 metres of a German trench. He had crashed in no man's land, and shells and mortar rounds were exploding nearby.

This sector was held at the time by the *4e régiment mixte de zouaves et de tirailleurs*. Four of its men tried to reach d'Arnoux from their front line 300 metres away, but one was killed and the others found themselves checked by barbed wire. They urged d'Arnoux to drag himself across to them, but he was unable to move. He later learned that a fracture of his spine had paralysed the lower part of his body.

That night, a ten-man patrol set off on a rescue mission, but had to withdraw after clashing with some Germans. Undaunted by the setback, a *sergent* crawled out to confirm that d'Arnoux was still alive and then took five other men to make a further attempt. By now it was growing light, but the rescuers were hidden by mist. On reaching d'Arnoux, they handed him a handkerchief. 'Put this in your mouth,' a *zouave* whispered. 'If you scream, we're dead.' At first, the men took it in turns to carry him on their backs as they stumbled through the shellholes. Then they hauled him along in a piece of tent canvas, and finally reached safety.

Once inside the trenches, d'Arnoux was whisked away on a stretcher. He forgot his agony. 'Quivers of elation revived my vigour, firing it up to a peak. Every fibre of my body thrilled to breaking point, and I wanted to shout for joy. . . . What did my wounds matter, whatever their gravity! I was saved. I was going to live.' He spent the next five years in hospital, but survived until he was 84.

Point D: German cemetery

Drive northwards up to the crossroads with the D18 CD. Continue straight ahead, along the road signposted for Fort de la Malmaison, and park at the entrance to the German military cemetery. Over 11,800 German soldiers are buried here, but they came from a later generation and died in the Second World War. This area saw heavy fighting in 1940, and the cemetery was created the following year. It was subsequently expanded as the remains of more men were transferred from further afield, and it now covers an area of 67,000 square metres, filling the whole space between the D18 CD and Fort de la Malmaison, the ruins of which are hidden amidst the trees on the northern side.

Point E: Fort de la Malmaison

It is possible to visit the ruined fort as part of a guided tour organized through the Caverne du dragon museum, though opportunities to do so are limited. Alternatively, you may wish to see its more-intact sister, Fort de Condé (Stop 29).

Built in 1876–83, Fort de la Malmaison dominated the western part

Smashed interior of Fort de la Malmaison in 1919.

of the Chemin des Dames and could shell the N2, the great high-road to Paris that ran just 1 km past its western flank. It became obsolete almost at once. In 1886 and 1894, it was used as a target for testing shells filled with a more powerful explosive called melinite. So effective were these shells that the French had to modernize their most important fortresses to give them additional protection. Less important forts, including those of Condé and La Malmaison, were decommissioned by 1914.

During the war, the location of Fort de la Malmaison made it a superb observation point. In May 1917, *Leutnant* Ebert of *Reserve-Feldartillerie-Regiment Nr 44* was sent there as an artillery observer:

> I was not exactly overjoyed, for I felt sure the coming days were going to be unpleasant. *Fort Malmaison* was a favourite target during the fighting on the Chemin des Dames, and was constantly under enemy artillery fire of heavy and very heavy calibres. . . . The observation from the fort was excellent. In fact, I do not remember ever having been in an observation point with a better view over our own lines and those of the enemy, and over the terrain further back.

During the preparation for the Malmaison offensive, the fort was so heavily bombarded that it looked like a volcano. The superstructure lay in ruins, but much still existed below ground, as did the perimeter ditch. The task of capturing it fell to the 3rd Battalion of the *4e zouaves*. Its commander was *Chef de bataillon* Henri Giraud, who distinguished himself by successfully escaping from German captivity in both world wars. For a time in 1943 he was joint president of the French Committee of National Liberation, but was outmanoeuvred politically by his rival, Charles de Gaulle.

To reach the fort, Giraud's battalion had to seize three successive trench-lines, the first two of which had been destroyed by the bombardment. At first, the fort was perfectly visible, for it was burning like a brazier after being hit by incendiary shells. It disappeared for a while behind a fold in the ground, causing some disorder among the *zouaves* as they passed through the craters in the darkness. The leading two companies of the battalion then separated, creating a gap that was filled by the support company. All three companies simultaneously reached the third German trench, which ran immediately in front of the fort, and the middle company mopped it up while the others formed two prongs and stormed the fort from the east and west. At 6.00 am, a *zouave* clambered to the top and triumphantly planted a flag on the ruins.

Point F: Monument to the *38e division*

Before driving further north, we shall make a brief excursion on foot along the Chemin des Dames. Start by walking to the crossroads with the D18 CD, where you will find a monument to the *38e division*. This point marked the eastern edge of the *RICM*'s attack zone. The righthand prong of the regiment had to sweep through the narrow strip of ground between here and the rim of the plateau just 140 metres away above the carrières de Bohéry.

To appreciate the difficulty of such a manoeuvre, you have to remember that the terrain looked drastically different at the time of the battle. The massive French bombardment may have levelled the foremost German trenches, but it also hindered the infantry and tanks by creating a sea of craters. 'The ground around the lines and in no man's land is nothing but a series of overlapping shell-holes,' noted Robert A. Donaldson of the American Ambulance Field Service. He visited this area three days after the attack, and wrote in his diary:

It looks, as far as the eye can see, as if it had been turned over time and again by a giant plough. The German first lines are so battered that it is almost impossible to tell them from the surrounding terrain. Nothing is left of the barbed wire save torn and buried tangles here and there. . . . The world on this plateau, as far as the eye can reach, is nothing but chaos. The marvel is how the attacking troops themselves ever advanced over it.

Even the actual roadway of the Chemin des Dames had disappeared. The writer Marcel Prévost described how he and his companions had to search for any trace of it as they picked their way across the cratered landscape on 24 October:

We must have crossed it without realizing. Let's go back and have a look around. Which of these shell-holes has swallowed it up? But we find it impossible to work out. We consult the map. Yes, we're right on it. The Chemin – the imperishably famous Chemin – used to branch off from the main road near this tree, and instantly head off to the south-east along the ridge-crest.
   'Here we are! Look!'
   One of us pointed out a thin layer of crushed stones, which looked like a slice of nougat embedded in the clay of a shell-hole.
   So that's where it used to be. That's what thousands of human beings lost their lives trying to capture.

Point G: *RICM* monument
From the crossroads, walk 550 metres westwards along the D18 CD until you come to the monument at the edge of the road. Unveiled in 1934, it commemorates the *Régiment d'infanterie coloniale du Maroc (RICM)*. At this point, you are due north of the ravine of the carrières de Bohéry, and it was in this area that the two prongs of the regiment linked up as they encircled the quarries. Look south and you will see the edge of the plateau just 200 metres away. The quarries are hidden amidst the trees on the slopes descending into the valley. Below, on the valley floor, is the village of Jouy.
   Inscribed on the monument is the citation earned by the *RICM*. This was its fifth citation in army orders, and in 1918 it increased the

Soldiers of the Régiment d'infanterie coloniale du Maroc after one of their most celebrated feats: the capture of Fort de Douaumont at Verdun in October 1916.

total to ten – more than any other regiment in the French army. The number of its citations entitled it to the double *fourragère*, or braided cord, which you can see carved at the top of the monument next to its unit decorations, the cross of the *Légion d'honneur*, the *Médaille militaire* and the *Croix de guerre* with ten palms on the ribbon.

Only a superbly trained unit could have carried out the *RICM*'s audacious sweep round both flanks of the carrières de Bohéry. Despite its name, the regiment was not composed of Moroccans. It was formed in August 1914 by uniting four battalions that had been helping to pacify the French protectorate of Morocco. These battalions consisted of volunteers drawn from various regiments of *infanterie coloniale*, whose anchor emblem can be seen on the monument.

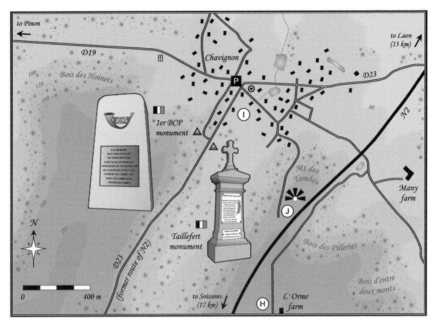

Chavignon.

Point H: L'Orme farm

Return to your car, and then drive from Fort de la Malmaison northwards along the road that follows the top of the spur. After 700 metres, pause at l'Orme farm, the ruins of which were taken by the *4e zouaves* during the second phase of the attack. (It was rebuilt in the same place after the war.) From a short distance south of the farm, you have a good view to the south-west and can see the white calvary of l'Ange Gardien 2.4 km away at the starting point of the Chemin des Dames (Stop 1).

Beyond l'Orme farm, the road slopes gently down to the north. At the time of the battle, it continued straight across the top of Mont des Tombes – the westernmost of the three stubs at the end of the spur. But that route was blocked when the new dual carriageway was built to enable the N2 to bypass the village of Chavignon. The road has therefore been diverted, and after an abrupt turn to the right it now passes down the eastern side of Mont des Tombes. While descending, look directly ahead and you will see Laon cathedral on the hilltop 12.5 km away. When you reach the T-junction at the foot of Mont des

Tombes, turn left and pass through the bridge under the N2. Continue until you come to the stop sign at the eastern outskirts of Chavignon. Turn right, and then, after 50 metres, go left at the fork in the road. When you reach the junction with the D23, turn left, continue into the centre of Chavignon, and park in the main square.

Point I: Chavignon

Walk over to the south-eastern side of the square to look at the local war memorial in front of the church. 'On 23 October 1917', records a plaque, 'the *4e régiment mixte zouaves et tirailleurs* had the honour and glory of retaking the village of Chavignon from the enemy.' One company of the regiment attacked Chavignon from the east, and another from the south in liaison with the *chasseurs à pied* of the neighbouring *43e division*. The village was fiercely defended and had to be taken step by step, but by 1.00 pm was wholly in French hands.

The *1er bataillon de chasseurs à pied* has its own monument at the southern end of the village. To reach it, go to the western corner of the main square, and walk 350 metres up the *rue des Ecoles*. The monument stands at the far end of the road and remembers the five officers and 112 other ranks of the battalion who fell on the Chemin des Dames in 1917.

The ruins of Chavignon.

Face directly away from the monument, and walk 50 metres along the road to the south-east until you reach the D23. The memorial on the opposite side of the D23 commemorates Frédéric Taillefert, one of the men of the *4e régiment mixte*. He was 21 years old when he died, and won a citation for going in front of the assault waves and firing an automatic rifle to ease their advance.

Point J: Mont des Tombes

From the southern side of the church, walk 300 metres south-eastwards along the *rue Saint Pierre*. Go up the *rue du 4ème zouaves et tirailleurs*. After 60 metres, you reach a fork. Take the lefthand road, the *impasse du Chemin des Dames*. It leads you uphill, past a water storage tank (a mound with a squat, white tower at the entrance), and then comes to an abrupt end where it has been cut off by the N2. At this point, take the grass track on the righthand side of the road, and follow it round to the left on to the open, grassy summit of Mont des Tombes. Enjoy the superb views from here, particularly over Chavignon to the north-west.

The summit of Mont des Tombes is narrower than it was at the time of the battle, for the N2 slices through the south-eastern side of the height in a deep cutting. Beyond this cutting, on much the same level as the ground on which you are standing, you can see l'Orme farm and the clump of trees that hides Fort de la Malmaison. Finally, face eastwards and look along the rear of the Chemin des Dames. The importance of the Malmaison sector becomes obvious when you see these commanding views.

NW

Heights north of Aisne–Marne canal

Chavignon today, seen from Mont des Tombes.

STOPS

Stops 1–10
Chemin des Dames:
Western Sector

Stop 1: Calvaire de l'Ange Gardien

This massive calvary marks the western end of the Chemin des Dames (the D18 CD) and serves as a memorial to the French soldiers who fell on the plateau. Made of reinforced concrete, it is 14 metres tall and was inaugurated in 1924. The road layout at this point has been changed, for the N2 has been turned into a dual carriageway and shifted to a slightly different route. Previously, it met the D18 CD at a simple T-junction at the foot of the calvary, but this has been replaced by a modernized junction 350 metres to the south-west. To reach the calvary from this new junction, take the turning signposted for Chavignon. This leads you along the D23 – the old route of the N2 – and you will see the calvary on your right. The name l'Ange Gardien is a relic of a long-vanished inn.

Calvaire de l'Ange Gardien.

Stop 2: Viewpoint of La Royère

The viewpoint lies 600 metres west of La Royère farm, at the place where the D152 joins the D18 CD from the north. A walkway slopes down into the ground to symbolize a trench, and contains information panels explaining the background to events in this sector. From the nearby mound, you can see the Chapelle Sainte-Berthe (Stop 3), and even Laon cathedral 14 km to the north-north-east. It was these sweeping views over the Ailette valley that made La Royère a point of friction throughout the summer of 1917, until the French finally gained full control of the area during the Malmaison offensive in October.

French soldiers who reached the crest of the Chemin des Dames were struck by the contrast between the desolate landscape in which they were fighting and the green countryside on the horizon. *Sous-lieutenant* Joseph Tézenas du Montcel of the *5e régiment d'infanterie coloniale* had spent so long living in the trenches below ground level that he was unused to such wide expanses stretching into the distance like an immense sea. In the ravaged zone the passing of the seasons hardly made any difference, whereas the unspoiled hills in the distance looked like the Promised Land.

Stop 3: Chapelle Sainte-Berthe

The Chapelle Sainte-Berthe lies on the spur that protrudes northwards from the Royère viewpoint into the Ailette valley. It now stands alone, but used to be enclosed within the farm of Saint-Martin. Both farm and chapel were destroyed in the war, and only the chapel was rebuilt (and not for the first time, for it had been devastated during the campaigns of 1814 and 1870–1).

Saint-Martin farm was seized by the *19e bataillon de chasseurs à pied* on 5 May 1917, as part of the more general French onslaught that day along the Chemin des Dames. A plaque on the chapel wall was dedicated by the battalion's descendant unit, the *19e groupe de chasseurs*. The battalion launched its attack from 800 metres south of the Chemin des Dames roadway, and stuck closely to the rolling barrage. Within forty minutes a company reached the farm and dashed in through the gateway, overcoming resistance with the suddenness of its irruption. 'In the distance', recorded the battalion war diary, 'the towers of Laon cathedral grew distinct. The men were fired up with enthusiasm, and the officers had trouble holding them back.'

One of the plaques at the Chapelle Sainte-Berthe.

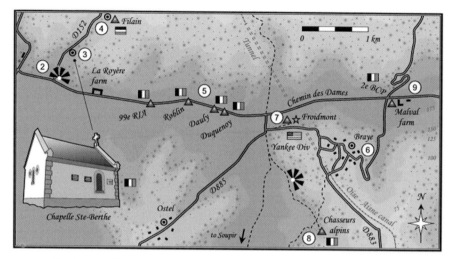

La Royère and Braye.

The success of the attack left the *chasseurs* out on a limb, exposed to fire from both flanks, and Saint-Martin farm was soon reduced to smoking ruins. The *19e bataillon* was relieved during the night of 7/8 May, but returned to this sector later in the month.

Two other plaques commemorate units that fought here during the Malmaison offensive in October 1917. (The chapel was near the eastern edge of the attack front.) One of these units was the *283e régiment*, which lost around half its strength on the first day of the offensive. The plaque to the *288e régiment* urges passers-by to remember the fallen soldiers from the *département* of the Gers in south-western France. Regiments in peacetime drew their manpower from their local region, but as the war progressed the gaps caused by heavy casualties often had to be filled without taking account of the origin of the replacements. Nevertheless, the composition of the *288e* continued to reflect its pre-war identity even as late as 1917. Between 20 and 31 October, 47 officers and men of the regiment were killed on the Chemin des Dames. As many as one in four of them had been born in the *département* of the Gers, and about half of the total were natives of the wider region of Gascony.

Stop 4: Filain

As you enter the village of Filain along the D152 from the Chapelle

German monument at Filain.

Sainte-Berthe, take the first turning to the right and go up to the church. Face the northern side of the building, and on your left you will see a grassy route beneath the churchyard wall. Follow it on foot round to the eastern side, where you will find a monument erected by the Germans during the war and dedicated to the fallen of both sides. The inscription reads:

> Sleep, friend and foe, united in death in the protecting bosom of the earth, until the Lord awakens the spirits with his word of creation: 'Let there be'.

Stop 5: Roadside monuments

To the east of La Royère farm, you pass four French monuments dotted along a 1.2-km stretch of the D18 CD. All are on the southern edge of the road. The first monument honours the *99e régiment*, which particularly distinguished itself on 20 May 1917. On that day, it lost over

200 men killed, wounded or missing while holding the spur of La Bovelle, 9 km east of where you are standing. In 1927, the *99e* was converted to a mountain warfare unit – a *régiment d'infanterie alpine* – and in June 1940 it found itself fighting once more on the Chemin des Dames as it tried to contain the renewed German onslaught following the Dunkirk evacuation.

The next monument is dedicated to 19-year-old *Soldat* Jean Roblin of the *146e régiment*, and to the comrades who fell with him on 18 May 1917. During this period, both sides were carrying out a series of raids and small-scale attacks. Affixed to the monument is the cockade of the *Souvenir français*, the society founded in 1887 to preserve the memory of France's fallen soldiers.

The final two monuments commemorate *Soldat* Jean Dauly and *Aspirant* Marcel Duquenoy of the *350e régiment*, both of whom were 20 years old. During the French attacks on 5 May 1917, two battalions of

Roblin monument.   *Dauly monument.*

the *350e* were described in its war diary advancing 'as if on parade, inspiring admiration in all who were there to watch, and even moving them to tears of pride'. The attack reached the woods covering the northern slopes of the plateau, but the units were then cut off by German barrages and that afternoon started to come under counter-attacks, which were renewed the following day. The inscription on Dauly's monument explains that he was killed on 6 May in the wood north of the road. 'Mourned by his mother, by his entire family and by his comrades,' adds the inscription. 'Pray for him.' The monument to *Aspirant* Duquenoy, 150 metres further along the D18 CD, is a tribute from his parents. He went missing in the same wood where Dauly was killed.

Stop 6: Braye

Braye lies in a basin on the southern side of the Chemin des Dames. Park in the village centre – you will find a few spaces next to the *mairie* – so you can explore the area. (Stops 7 and 8 have to be visited on foot as they lie at the end of tracks.)

On 16 April 1917, the German front line jutted out in front of the Chemin des Dames to form a salient extending as far as the town of Vailly on the Aisne. After two days of French attacks, the Germans holding this salient fell back to the top of the plateau. The French advanced in pursuit and entered Braye on the morning of the 18th, but were checked by machine-gun fire on the slopes beyond the village. The front stabilized here, with the Germans dominating the basin from the higher ground.

In the south-western outskirts of Braye, you will find the start of a canal tunnel. The canal was built in the 1880s to link the Oise and Aisne rivers, though the tunnel entrance has been modernized. The tunnel is 2,365 metres long, and passes beneath the Chemin des Dames to emerge in the Ailette valley. Before the Nivelle offensive, the Germans used the canal to bring supplies by motorboat to their front-line units, until a French bombardment on 19 March 1917 damaged the locks and released the water. 'What a distressing sight!' wrote a French artillery officer later that year. 'This canal is just a bed of stagnant mud, and on its bottom are lying rows of smashed barges that were caught there by the war and sunk with their loads.' The Germans blew up the tunnel entrance in the early hours of 18 April when they abandoned the Vailly salient. While they were making the preparations for the demolition, an officer of *Reserve-Infanterie-Regiment Nr 440* was killed 50 metres inside the tunnel by a shell splinter that flew in from the entrance.

Stop 7: Carrière de Froidmont
The now-vanished farm of Froidmont was a formidable German strongpoint. Perched on the upper slopes of the plateau, it loomed over the Braye basin and was attacked in vain by the *12e division* on 5 and 6 May 1917. To reach the site of the farm from Braye, walk westwards along the *rue Marquette de Signy* and up out of the valley. After 1 km, turn sharp right on to a track that heads back in an easterly direction. After 200 metres, the track bends round and reaches an open area, at the edge of which is a sandbagged structure. This is the entrance to the carrière de Froidmont, an underground quarry containing some remarkable artwork carved by soldiers during the war, which can be visited by prior arrangement.

Next to the quarry entrance is a memorial to the US 26th Division. After the United States entered the war in April 1917, the 26th was one of the first divisions to be sent to France. It was known as the Yankee Division since it came from New England and was formed from the National Guard of all six of the region's states: Connecticut, Maine, Massachusetts, New Hampshire, Rhode Island and Vermont. Even after arriving in France, the division needed several months of training before it could be used in action. Early in 1918, it spent a spell on the Chemin des Dames, which had become a quiet sector after finally being abandoned by the Germans the previous autumn. As a French general noted, the sector could be held by second-rate units: 'Young troops, such as those of the US divisions, would find every training facility there, owing to the variety of terrain and the distance separating the [opposing] lines.' The 26th Division was split up into separate elements and integrated with French regiments, so it was able to gain some front-line experience under supervision. The 26th Division was assigned to hold the area west of the Oise–Aisne canal tunnel, and remained in this sector from early February 1918 until the middle of March. Hostilities were normally limited to patrols, harassing fire and the occasional minor raid, and the division's losses amounted to just nineteen officers and men.

Stop 8: *Chasseurs alpins* monument

Be aware that this next stop is a 4-km walk there-and-back from the carrière de Froidmont, and that the route can not be driven. Start by rejoining the minor road from Braye that runs past the southern side of the *carrière*. Walk up this road, heading west, until it bends to the right. Turn off to the left at this bend. Immediately afterwards, turn left again on to the track leading south and follow the signs for the '*27 BCA*'. After 250 metres you will need to turn left once more, but thereafter you should simply follow the track along the top of the wooded slopes of the plateau until you come to the monument.

Inaugurated in 1947, this is a memorial to two battalions of crack mountain infantry, the famous *chasseurs alpins*. The two units – the *27e*

'In memory of our dead': the chasseurs alpins monument.

bataillon and its reserve formation, the *67e* – both fought on the Chemin des Dames during 1917, notably in the Malmaison offensive as part of the *66e division*. In November 1918, the *27e* had its *fanion* (a small flag) decorated with the coveted red *fourragère*, as a result of having been cited six times in army orders. It was the first *chasseur* battalion to obtain this distinction, and was congratulated in person by the head of the government, Georges Clémenceau. Since Clémenceau was known as 'The Tiger', the battalion acquired a tiger emblem to supplement the traditional hunting horn of the *chasseurs*.

The reason why the monument stands in such a remote location is that it marks the site of the command post of *Lieutenant* Jacques Romieu, a company commander of the *27e bataillon*, who was killed here on 6 June 1940. By a quirk of fate, the battalion had ended up fighting on the Chemin des Dames in both world wars. You can still see the remains of defensive positions behind the monument, and the Oise–Aisne canal below in the distance.

Stop 9: Malval farm

Malval farm used to stand 200 metres further north, on the slopes that descend into the Ailette valley, but was rebuilt after the war alongside the D18 CD. A stone cross at its north-western corner commemorates the 180 men of the *2e bataillon de chasseurs à pied* who fell while attacking Malval on 5 May 1917.

The battalion belonged to the *11e division* – the renowned *Division de fer*, or 'Iron Division' – and launched its attack from the southern edge of the Chemin des Dames plateau, some 500 metres south of the D18 CD. At 9.00 am, *Capitaine* René Simonin, the commander of the 1st Company, gave the signal to go over the top. Since a shouted command might have alerted the Germans, he instead waved a white *fanion* (a small flag) made from the silk of a parachute flare and inscribed in blue pencil with *Sursum corda* – a Latin phrase commonly used during the celebration of masses, meaning 'Lift up your hearts!'

The attack was meant to consist of two phases. After an initial bound to seize the German trenches alongside the D18 CD, the *chasseurs* were to pause for three-quarters of an hour to ensure they were properly supported on their flanks. Only then were they to advance beyond the crest to seize Malval. But the men were so eager that they simply dashed onwards without pausing. 'The *chasseurs*, mesmerized by the final objective, were lured by Malval farm as if by a lover,' reported a *sous-lieutenant*. At 9.30 am, just half-an-hour after the start of the attack, the battalion commander, *Commandant* Georges Mellier, received a message from *Capitaine* Simonin announcing that he was at the farm.

'I embrace you,' Mellier replied. 'Hold on, you have our support. I'm letting the artillery know. Hurrah for the 1st Company!' Yet his enthusiasm was premature, for the *chasseurs* were now exposed out in front of the neighbouring units. They were counter-attacked, took heavy losses from machine-gun fire and had to fall back behind the

Malval farm: monument to the 2e bataillon de chasseurs à pied.

D18 CD. *Capitaine* Simonin was among those killed. *Commandant* Mellier blamed him for the setback and wrote in his report:

> *Capitaine* Simonin . . . has paid a heavy price for having ignored the strict order he was given not to go beyond the objective set for the end of the first bound – an order that I went and personally reminded him of . . . a few minutes before zero hour. The battalion has been the victim of the ardour of this officer, who became carried away and thereby carried his unit away with him.

The fallen included *Sous-lieutenant* Henri de Bonnand-Montaret, who had enlisted as a volunteer at the age of 19 and served in the cavalry before joining the *2e bataillon de chasseurs à pied* in February 1917. The monument is dedicated to him in particular, and quotes an extract from one of his letters: 'Frenchmen, fear nothing, but pray to God for the battalion.'

Stop 10: Paissy

Paissy is an unusual place, strung along a 1.5-km stretch of road as it curves round the hillside. *Creutes* in the cliff-face behind the houses have been used as storage spaces, or even as troglodyte homes. Several information boards can be found at the western end of the village, where the main street is joined by the *rue de l'Eglise*. They explain that the *249e régiment* (part of the *18e corps*) occupied this sector from June 1915 to April 1916. The regimental staff was established in the *creutes*, whose entrances were protected by the cliff from German artillery fire. Inhabitants also used the *creutes* for refuge during these early years of the war, and schoolchildren even had lessons in them. Walk up the *rue de l'Eglise* to reach the church, where you will find the graves of several British and French soldiers.

Stop 11

Cerny

Cerny has been rebuilt on the summit of the Chemin des Dames, but used to stand 400 metres further north at the start of the descent into the valley. The village was difficult to capture and hold, for any attackers who passed over the crest and into the Cerny basin lacked effective fire support as they could no longer be seen by their own artillery observers. During the First Battle of the Aisne, for example, Lieutenant Colonel John Ponsonby of the 1/Coldstream Guards was cut off at Cerny on 14 September 1914 with around 100 British soldiers, and was fortunate to make it back to friendly lines after dark with the remnants of his party.

WHAT HAPPENED

On 16 April 1917, this sector was attacked by the *153e division* (from the *20e corps*), which made some of the deepest French gains anywhere that day. To the west of Cerny, the division progressed 2 km and reached the roadway of the Chemin des Dames, taking the observation point of the Arbre de Cerny. But the eastern wing of the division was checked by the ruins of a *sucrerie*, or sugar-beet refinery, which lay at the centre of a nest of entrenchments. The *sucrerie* remained a point of friction during the weeks that followed. By creating a bulge in the front line, it allowed German machine-gunners to fire into the flank and rear of nearby attacks.

The next major French assault on Cerny came on 5 May. The *93e régiment* (part of the *21e division* of the *11e corps*) attacked with two battalions side-by-side. Elements of the lefthand battalion passed beyond their objective and penetrated into the ruins of Cerny, but were unable to hold the village. The battalion on the right overran the trenches to its fore so swiftly that it trapped part of *Infanterie-Regiment Nr 77* inside a tunnel. The Germans tried to dig their way out, only to find that the new exit they made was also blocked by fire. Further

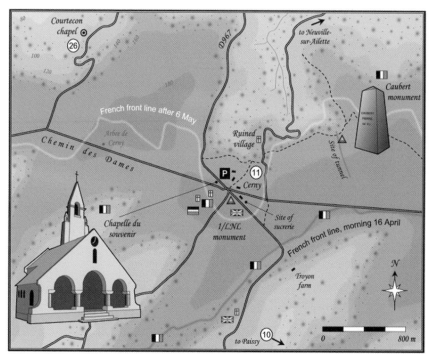

Cerny.

resistance was pointless, and the survivors surrendered as the French were threatening to gas the tunnel. In this righthand battalion of the *93e*, the *adjudant-major*, or executive officer, was *Capitaine* Jean de Lattre. Better known as *Général* de Lattre de Tassigny, he commanded the *1ère armée* during the Second World War and then the French forces in Indochina, and was made a *maréchal* following his death in 1952.

The French attacks in April–May had carved out salients on either side of Cerny, placing it in permanent danger of being pinched out. From the rim of the plateau east of the village, the French could see into the basin and fire at any movements. But during the summer the Germans gradually eliminated both the salients and drove the French back to the Chemin des Dames roadway or even beyond it. Only when the Germans abandoned the entire plateau at the beginning of November were the French finally able to occupy Cerny.

WHAT TO SEE

Cerny has become the main focal point on the battlefield for ceremonies of remembrance. This is partly because of its symbolic importance as the supposed birthplace of Saint Rémi, the Bishop of Reims who baptised Clovis, the first king to unite the Franks. The village is also easy to reach, lying as it does midway along the Chemin des Dames, at the crossroads with the D967, which runs southwards from Laon all the way to Château-Thierry on the Marne river.

Chapelle du souvenir

Elsewhere on the Western Front – on the battlefields of Verdun, the Marne, Artois and the Vosges – the French nation built four great monuments to its fallen soldiers. The omission of the Chemin des Dames owed much to the controversies surrounding the Nivelle offensive. Almost all the memorials on the plateau have been the result of private initiatives by individuals or associations. The largest of these private memorials is the chapel of remembrance at Cerny, erected by the *Union nationale des combattants* – the association founded at the end

Tributes inside the chapel at Cerny.

of 1918 for French veterans, war widows and orphans. The chapel was inaugurated only in 1951 after two decades of delays and abandoned projects, and is just a modest, scaled-back part of the memorial that was originally planned.

The walls inside the chapel are covered with plaques. Some have been placed here by units or associations of veterans, while others are personal tributes to individuals such as *Capitaine* Edouard Lefranc, the commander of a Senegalese battalion in Marchand's division (Tour I). Not all the men commemorated in the chapel actually died on the Chemin des Dames. *Soldat* Georges Moncourtois of the *67e régiment* fell 140 km away in the *département* of the Meuse in 1914, but he has a plaque since he was born at Vassogne, less than 5 km from Cerny. At the time of writing, the chapel contains seventy-five plaques. Just one is dedicated to a German soldier, and it was added as recently as 2011. The soldier in question, *Unteroffizier* Eduard Miles of *Reserve-Infanterie-Regiment Nr 110*, fell when the French conquered the plateau de Californie – also known as the *Winterberg* – on 5 May 1917 (Tour IV).

Outside the chapel

Near the chapel are two military cemeteries: one French and one German. Over 12,500 men are buried here. The lantern of the dead in front of the chapel was added in the 1960s. (Towers with lanterns were

Cerny: monument to the 38e division, with the memorial chapel in the background.

often built in medieval France, their apparent purpose being to guide the souls of the departed.) Next to the lantern is a memorial to the renowned *38e division,* which captured Fort de la Malmaison in October 1917 (Tour V). Among those who served in the division was a Jesuit priest and stretcher-bearer, *Caporal* Pierre Teilhard de Chardin, who later became an influential writer and philosopher. One of the plaques in the chapel explains that his experiences on the Chemin des Dames in 1917 helped shape his thinking about the future of mankind.

Loyal North Lancashire Regiment

The ornate column 50 metres south-east of the crossroads commemorates the men of the 1/Loyal North Lancashire Regiment who fell during the war. The battalion was heavily engaged here during the First Battle of the Aisne. It formed part of the 1st Division, whose attempt to seize the top of the plateau on 14 September 1914 was narrowly foiled by the Germans. Some of the men who died that day are buried at the Commonwealth cemetery of Vendresse, 1.5 km to the south along the D967.

Such was the devastation on the Chemin des Dames immediately after the war that identifying the right site on which to erect the monument proved unusually difficult. The roads provided no guidance, as they had been destroyed by the shelling. The official map showing land ownership added to the confusion as it was more than eighty years out of date, and few inhabitants could be asked for guidance since Cerny consisted of just two wooden huts, and its mayor lived at Soissons.

1/Loyal North Lancashire monument at Cerny.

The Loyal North Lancashire Regiment has now disappeared as a result of army reductions, and its successor unit is The Duke of Lancaster's Regiment. Some 200 metres south-east of the monument is the site of the *sucrerie,* which is marked by a sign at the edge of the D967.

Destroyed village

The remnants of old Cerny are still visible inside the forest, and can be visited on foot. From the central crossroads of the rebuilt village, a grass track leads north-eastwards down the slope. After 340 metres, you will come to a junction with a narrow, lateral road. Turn right on to this road, and follow it as it bends round to the left 100 metres further on. It then descends northwards to the local civilian cemetery, which marks the site of the old churchyard.

Fifty metres south of the cemetery, a path leads into the forest from the western side of the road and meanders through the old village. Afterwards, return to the start of the path and walk 75 metres up the road, heading south away from the cemetery. Then turn left on to a dirt track and and go 750 metres in an easterly direction until the track starts to bend round to the north. At the top of the embankment on your right is a stone obelisk commemorating *Soldat* Pierre Caubert, who fell at Cerny on 8 May 1917. He belonged to the *64e régiment*, which formed part of the *21e division*. The monument also bears the name of *Soldat* Auguste Vinet of the same regiment, who died from his wounds at Amiens in October 1914.

Stop 12

Caverne du Dragon

Beneath the fertile fields on the top of the Chemin des Dames plateau lies a layer of white limestone riddled with the underground quarries known locally as *creutes*. The Caverne du dragon has become the most legendary of all these grottoes, partly because its capture by the French on 25 June 1917 generated such a blaze of publicity. Propagandists exploited the success to try to restore the French army's shaken morale. Today, the cavern is one of the most popular tourist attractions in the *département* of the Aisne, and provides a remarkable glimpse into the experiences of the soldiers who lived under the Chemin des Dames.

Hidden dangers

Creutes had multiple functions, ranging from the storage of farmers' tools to the extraction of limestone for use as a building material. During the war, they protected soldiers from the rain, cold and shelling. They were obvious locations for command posts and dressing stations, and could accommodate units close to the front line in a surprising degree

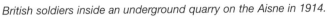

British soldiers inside an underground quarry on the Aisne in 1914.

A partially demolished creute.

of comfort. The Caverne du dragon boasted latrines and sleeping quarters, a water source, a first-aid post, stores of food, equipment and ammunition, and even electric lighting provided by petrol-driven generators.

Yet *creutes* were also overcrowded and infested with rats. The air was stale and humid, and water often dripped from the roof. 'The atmosphere is pervaded with every kind of foul stench,' wrote a French military chaplain. 'The smell of tobacco, sweat, slop-buckets and food grips your throat and makes you feel sick. What a breeding-ground for fleas.' Shut off from outside, the men did not notice whether it was night or day. The interior was lit by an eerie, greenish-white light – if the generator was working at all.

Hidden dangers lurked inside *creutes*. If the entrances were smashed by shells or blocked by machine-gun fire, the garrison could find itself trapped. Grenades might be dropped down air-shafts, or flamethrowers used against the exits. Poisonous gas was heavier than air, so it tended to sink into underground spaces. Even the protection against bombardment could turn out to be illusory, and the loss of life could be sickeningly high if the roof did collapse under the impact of a heavy shell. On 25 September 1914, nearly thirty officers and men of the 1/Queen's Own Cameron Highlanders died when they were entombed inside a *creute*.

WHAT HAPPENED

The Caverne du dragon was initially known by the bland and anonymous name of La Creute. It was held by the French until January 1915, when they lost their remaining foothold on this sector of the plateau to a German attack. Over the next two years the Germans enlarged the cavern and dug a tunnel linking it to a smaller *creute* 90 metres away on the northern slopes of the Chemin des Dames. The tunnel made it possible for supplies and relief units to be brought into

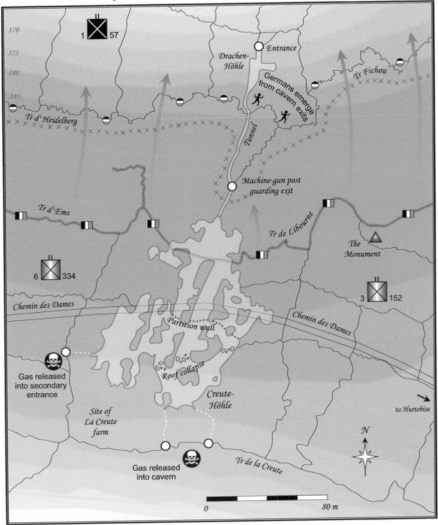

Caverne du dragon, 25 June 1917.

the cavern under cover, without having to pass over the top of the plateau to the exposed southern entrances. The small, northern *creute* was called the *Drachen-Höhle*, or dragon's cave, and eventually the entire complex became known to the French as the Caverne du dragon.

At the start of the Nivelle offensive, the Germans held the southern edge of the plateau, with the cavern right behind them, but by early May 1917 they had been driven back beyond the geographical crest. The French front line now lay directly above the cavern – a situation that made both sides uneasy. The Germans inside the cavern abandoned the southern part and sealed it off with a loopholed wall in case of any attempt to break in or blow it up. The French took a similar precaution, blocking the main southern exit from the cavern with sandbags and a machine-gun lest a sudden sortie by the garrison emerged behind their first line.

Just 250 metres to the north-east of the Caverne du dragon was one of the most sensitive locations on the Chemin des Dames. Part of the plateau jutted northwards like a finger, forming a protrusion called the Doigt d'Hurtebise. Although held by the French, it was a constant source of concern to them, for it constituted a thin and dangerously exposed salient. On the evening of 16 June it fell to a Bavarian attack. The *Monument* – the central, dominant point on this part of the Chemin des Dames – was now dangerously exposed right behind the French front line.

To the French, the loss of the Doigt d'Hurtebise was intolerable not simply from a tactical point of view but also for reasons of morale and prestige. They decided to mount a powerful attack, designed not simply to recover the lost salient but also to gain space on its western flank so as to improve the original position. In order to be secure, they needed to establish themselves on the northern rim of the plateau, from where they could look down and see the whole of the descent into the Ailette valley. This would enable them to spot any preparations for a surprise counter-attack being made at the foot of the plateau. By dominating the slopes, the French could also isolate the Caverne du Dragon by keeping its northern entrance covered by machine-gun fire.

Gas attack

The French had to mount their attack soon, so as to pre-empt any additional German onslaught that might capture the *Monument* itself.

The attack was entrusted to the *164e division* and scheduled for 25 June. It would be made by a battalion of the *334e régiment* on the left, a battalion of the crack *152e régiment* in the centre, and a composite unit of *groupes francs* (specially trained assault and raiding detachments) against the Doigt on the right.

One of the biggest problems in planning the attack was that nobody knew what exactly lay inside the Caverne du dragon. The commander of the *164e division* wrote:

> Despite the reconnaissance reports that I have found in my files – and some of them seem rather fanciful to me – we know absolutely nothing definite about the interior layout of the grotto. Is there or is there not a partition? If such a wall does exist, is it constructed of cement or of sandbags? Does it or does it not have an opening? None of these questions can be answered. It hardly seems advisable to send reconnaissances into the grotto, since they would fall into a trap if it turns out to be occupied. Similar attempts that were made in the past are said to have failed bloodily.

The solution was to release poisonous gas into the cavern through entrances located behind the French front line. Gas was an ingenious means of reconnoitring the cavern. If the interior was completely blocked by a partition wall, the gas would be forced back, and the French could simply seal off the entrances. But if the wall had openings, the gas would gradually fill the cavern and force any Germans who were inside to emerge from the northern exit, which was visible from a French listening post on the top of the plateau.

Preparations were made during the night before the attack. A detachment of just over fifty men from a specialist gas unit, Company 31/4 of the *1er régiment du génie*, fixed pipes to bottles of liquid phosgene and passed the tubes through sandbag barriers at two entrances. At 4.00 am on the 25th, the phosgene started to be released. By the time the engineers had finished seventy-five minutes later, 200 cubic metres of the gas were seeping through the cavern – enough to fill between 7 and 9 per cent of a typical modern-day hot-air balloon.

One of the entrances to the Caverne du dragon.

Tense wait

As the artillery continued its bombardment, the infantry prepared to attack that evening. *Médecin-major* Jean-Gabriel Chagnaud of the *152e régiment* waited tensely. 'All day, we passed the time as best we could,' he wrote, 'a bit nervously, by refining the details of a preparation that was already perfect.'

Zero hour was fixed for 6.05 pm. Some flamethrower teams took the precaution of lighting their weapons three minutes early, in case they did not work the first time. But the black smoke rising into the air from these jets of fire was mistaken for the attack signal. The French infantry jumped off ahead of schedule and only by sheer luck escaped being caught in a hail of 75mm shells unleashed in the final minute of the artillery preparation.

The start of the assault triggered a German barrage, which soon hid the plateau in smoke, dust and explosions. 'Shells were landing everywhere,' recalled *Gefreiter* Nehrdich of *Infanterie-Regiment Nr 57.* 'The din made it impossible to shout, and smoke drifted over the area. It was absolute bedlam.' In a single, unbroken rush, the French took their objectives. Although some German machine-guns had to be knocked out with flamethrowers or 37mm cannon, resistance on the whole was weak.

As for the Caverne du dragon, its northern entrance had been blocked by the preliminary bombardment and the Germans inside were trapped when the attack overran the alternative exits. Several French soldiers claimed credit for extracting the haul of 200–250 prisoners from the underground lair, including a chaplain of the *152e régiment* called Jean Py. It was he who received most recognition, but the cavern had so many exits that persuading the Germans to surrender took the efforts of a number of men from both the *152e* and the *334e*.

The attack was a clear-cut success, for as well as capturing the cavern, the French cleared the top of the plateau and now dominated the Ailette valley. They lost only around 320 officers and men killed, wounded or missing, mostly to artillery fire before and after the attack rather than from opposition during the attack itself.

Inside the cavern

Gefreiter Nehrdich described the interior of the Caverne du dragon several days before the attack:

> The *Drachen-Höhle* is very spacious, and can accommodate well over a battalion. We entered the cavern through an entrance on the northern side, which it was obvious had already been demolished several times by shelling. An exit led to our most advanced trench above, while another exit further back ended behind the French line. In front of the latter passageway stood a barricade, where our two machine-guns were posted with a floodlight in order to check the enemy should they break in. . . . My 'bed' was a plank with a sack of dried vegetables as a pillow.

French soldiers inside the Caverne du dragon.

The cavern contained far fewer troops than it might have done. Two companies were withdrawn just three days before the attack, lest they became trapped inside. Those Germans who remained on the morning of the 25th were in the northern part, behind the partition wall that stretched from the floor to the ceiling. When the French released the phosgene into the cavern, it was detected by look-outs guarding openings in the wall. The gas oxidized metal objects and forced the Germans to keep their masks on, but was not concentrated enough to be really effective, for the French had failed to realize the extent to which the Germans had enlarged the cavern during the previous couple of years. When the troops inside surrendered, it was not the gas in itself that forced them to do so. What did influence their decision was an awareness that they would be unable to withstand a further emission.

Aftermath
One month after the fall of the Caverne du dragon, a German attack drove back the French on the surface of the plateau and managed to break into the underground complex. Each side ended up holding part of the main cavern, separated by a barricade. By early September, the French had managed to regain the part they had lost, except for some of the tunnel. The sector became quieter later that month, and the Germans abandoned the Chemin des Dames at the beginning of November.

Caverne du dragon museum.

WHAT TO SEE

The Caverne du dragon became a visitor attraction even during the war – within days of its capture in June 1917 it was being explored by French soldiers. *Médecin-major* Chagnaud visited on the 27th after the remaining gas had been cleared from inside:

> Pulling myself along on my belly, I slid and tumbled down into a hole. I then went along a partly collapsed tunnel, and emerged into an initial chamber that was cluttered with enormous blocks that had fallen from the roof. I clambered through a newly made opening in a wall, and arrived at last in the grotto proper. . . . One by one the men of my detachment jumped down on to the fine sand that formed the ground, and we gazed about in amazement.

The cavern was turned into a museum in 1969. It reopened in 1999 after a major renovation of the site, which involved the construction of the innovative glass-and-concrete building that you see on the surface today. Visits underground are by guided tour only. Allow one-and-a-half hours, and take a coat since the temperature in the cavern is just 12 degrees centigrade. Most of the commentaries are in French, so check on the time of the English tour before you arrive.

Outside the museum, a couple of monuments at the edge of the D18 CD commemorate the *164e division* and one of its units, the *41e bataillon de chasseurs à pied*. (Other monuments in this area are covered in Tour I.) To commemorate the capture of the cavern, the *164e division* adopted the dragon as its emblem, and became the *Division du dragon*. It had been formed in November 1916, but had its first real baptism of fire on the Chemin des Dames. During the division's 26-month existence, its losses amounted to over 12,000 men. One-quarter of them were incurred in the three months it spent on the Chemin des Dames in 1917. This was the period that truly forged the division into a cohesive formation. 'The *164e division* has won a fine share of glory on the Aisne,' its commander wrote. 'The general in command of the division is proud to have been placed at the head of such troops.'

Stops 13–20
Chemin des Dames:
Eastern Sector

Stop 13: Napoleon's statue

To the east of Hurtebise farm, the high ground broadens out to form
the triangular plateau de Vauclair. Drive along the D18 CD to the north-
eastern end of this plateau, and you will find a track leading 75 metres
southwards across the fields to a statue of Napoleon. During the Battle
of Craonne in 1814, he supposedly used a windmill at this spot as an
observation post. The dilapidated mill – the moulin de Vauclair – was
destroyed during the First World War, but its location remained tactically
important because of the commanding nature of the ground. This point

Plateau de Vauclair.

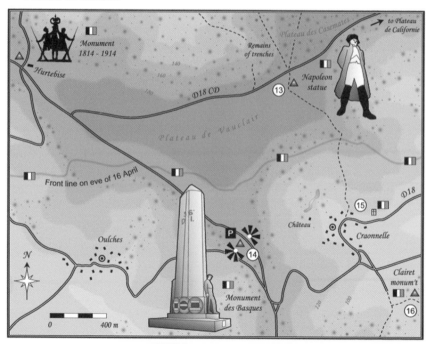

Remains of a trench in the forest north of Napoleon's statue.

was seized on 16 April 1917 by the *43e régiment*, which belonged to the *1er corps* on the left wing of the *5e armée*.

From Napoleon's statue, walk back to the D18 CD and continue directly ahead, across the road and down the track that descends into the forest on the far side. (Ignore the other track that branches off to the right, signposted for St Victor.) Within the forest, several information boards indicate the remains of trenches and can be found by following the wooden posts marked with the emblem of a dismounted cyclist.

Stop 14: *Monument des Basques*

Standing at the southernmost tip of the plateau de Vauclair is one of the most distinctive of all the monuments on the Chemin des Dames. This 14-metre high obelisk commemorates the *36e division*, which served in this sector from September 1914 to April 1916 as part of the *18e corps*.

Monument des Basques.

After fighting at Verdun, it returned in 1917 and captured the plateau de Californie (Tour IV).

The base of the monument records the *départements* from which the division's units were drawn at the start of the war. They came from the Basque country in south-western France. The solitary statue depicts a man in the clothes of a Basque civilian, gazing south-westwards towards his homeland. French wartime propaganda made much of the grenade-throwing feats of the Basques, and attributed this prowess to experience they gained from playing their traditional sport, *pelote*. Similar claims were made in Britain about the usefulness of cricket: 2/Lieutenant Tom Adlam of the 7/Bedfords won the Victoria Cross at the Somme in 1916 by hurling grenades with skills he had honed as a cricketer.

The monument was inaugurated in 1928. Its sculptor, Claude Grange, was himself a veteran of the Chemin des Dames – he took part in the Nivelle offensive as a company commander in the *2e corps d'armée colonial*.

Stop 15: Craonnelle

The Germans captured Craonnelle on 26 September 1914. Realizing that the low-lying village was too exposed to be held permanently, they abandoned it two nights later after setting it on fire. Almost four years elapsed before it fell once more, during the German offensive on 27 May 1918. This sector was defended by the British 50th Division, and part of the 4/Yorkshires made a brief stand amidst the ruined houses of Craonnelle.

The village has been rebuilt in its original location. In its centre you will find a stone water fountain that stood here during the war. Futher east, on the road to Craonne, is a French military cemetery containing the remains of nearly 4,000 men, including *Soldat* Clairet in Grave 585 and *Capitaine* Marqué in Grave 89 (see Stops 16 and 17).

Craonnelle during the war.

Fontaine du poilu: the water fountain at Craonnelle.

Stop 16: Clairet monument

Soldat Fernand Clairet belonged to the *1er régiment* (part of the *1er corps*), which attacked Craonne between 16 and 19 April 1917. His monument stands beside a track 600 metres south-east of Craonnelle. The inscription records the wrong date of death: he actually died on 18 April, at the age of 30. You will find his grave in the military cemetery of Craonnelle.

Stop 17: Chapelle Notre-Dame de Beaumarais

This small, roadside oratory 1 km north-east of Craonnelle bears several plaques. One of them is a tribute to *Monseigneur* Pierre Douillard, who served in this area as a chaplain with the *73e régiment* and later became the Bishop of Soissons. Also remembered is *Capitaine* Jean Henri Marqué of the *152e régiment*, who was killed by a shellburst on 30 May 1917. He is buried in the military cemetery of Craonnelle.

Stop 18: Menéteau and Barreau calvary

Both the next two stops are linked to the *36e régiment*, which occupied the Bois de Beaumarais for almost five months from December 1914. (The regiment formed part of the *3e corps*, within the *5e armée*.) The first stop is a calvary at the north-eastern edge of the wood, opposite La Renaissance farm. To reach it, drive to the crossroads 2.5 km south of Corbeny, where the D19 meets the D889, and then walk 600 metres along the track that leads west-north-west, keeping the edge of the wood on your left.

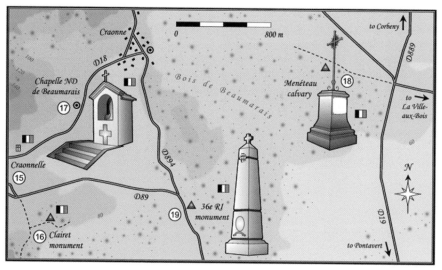

Bois de Beaumarais.

On 25 January 1915, four men of the *36e régiment* were killed when this sector came under intense German shelling. Among them was 26-year-old *Sergent* Georges Menéteau, who had given up a well-paid career before the war in order to enter a seminary. He was mobilized in August 1914, since the clergy had no exemption from military service under the French Republic's secular laws. The opening weeks of campaigning landed him in hospital with exhaustion, but he wanted to rejoin his comrades, and his opportunity came at the end of October when he volunteered to replace an NCO from the regimental depot – an older, family man – who had been picked to go to the front.

Ménéteau served in the Bois de Beaumarais. He was nicknamed the *petit sergent du bon Dieu* – the 'Good Lord's little sergeant' – and he organized a night of worship in the trenches just a few weeks before his death. The afternoon of 25 January found him encouraging the men in the trenches under the German bombardment. 'Come on, my children,' he told them, 'we are going to say the rosary.' As he prayed, a shell exploded between him and *Soldat* Emile Barreau, killing them both. One of Ménéteau's friends, a fellow *sergent*, recalled his cheerfulness. 'He died with a smile on his lips, and his rosary in his hands.' Ménéteau, he added, had done an enormous amount of good there – both to him personally and to all the soldiers of the company, who greatly loved him. 'I think that Georges Ménéteau was a saint,' he wrote. 'God has taken him from us.'

Ménéteau was initally buried with Barreau in a small, provisional cemetery, but their remains were found and reinterred at the foot of this calvary in 1924.

Stop 19: Monument to the *36e régiment*
The monument stands 130 metres south of the junction between the D89 and the D894, and is dedicated to the 3,375 officers, NCOs and men of the *36e régiment* who fell during the war. Among the names listed are those of Ménéteau and Barreau.

It was here that one of the regiment's officers, *Commandant* Georges-Théodore Chassery, had a rustic chapel erected in April 1915. 'I am having my chapel built, dedicated to Joan of Arc,' he wrote. 'Our chaplain can no longer contain his joy at the thought of having a church-cathedral measuring 8 metres by 4, with an altar and steeple.' Constructed of wattle, it served as a memorial for the men of the 3rd Battalion who had fallen in this sector.

At this stage in the war, much of the Bois de Beaumarais remained idyllic. 'This forest was an enchanting place, a dreamed-of paradise,' wrote one Frenchman. 'Its springtime charm and the luxuriant foliage of its trees extended from the banks of the Aisne to the foothills of

Craonne, until [in 1917] it was massacred by the shells and died a prolonged and agonizing death.'

Chassery's chapel was inaugurated on 27 April 1915. But he had learned that his regiment was due to be sent elsewhere. 'My heart is breaking at the idea of leaving these woods, to which I have become deeply attached.' He consoled himself with the thought that he was being summoned to defend France at some other location, and that he would do his duty to the very end. The *36e régiment* left the Bois de Beaumarais in the middle of May. Chassery hoped to return after the war so he could make a pilgrimage to his chapel, but four weeks later he was dead. He was mortally wounded on 9 June during the French offensive in Artois. 'My only regret is being unable to lead you to the end,' he said after being hit. 'Long live France!'

Stop 20: Chevreux

The hamlet of Chevreux was destroyed during the war and has never been rebuilt. It stood at the eastern foot of the plateau de Californie, at the point where the D18 CD crosses the D19. A monument at the crossroads pays tribute to the *8e* and *208e régiments*. These were sister units, for during the army's mobilization at the start of the war each active infantry regiment created a twin composed of reservists recalled to the colours. The active regiment provided a cadre of officers and NCOs as a skeleton around which to form the reservist unit, which took the same regimental number but with the addition of 200.

Both regiments belonged to the *2e division* of the *1er corps*, and on 16 April 1917 attacked the German front line 850 metres south-east of Chevreux. One of the officers in the *8e régiment* was *Sous-lieutenant* Louis Mairet. On the eve of the action, he wrote a final letter to his parents:

> My twenty-third birthday looks set to be a great day. . . . I'm calm, for everything is in order. Besides, I have no niggling feelings of foreboding . . . I really do hope, once I've washed off this smoke, that I'll come to see you in good health and spirits. It won't be long. I embrace you with all my heart, and bid you a big 'Farewell!' for I truly hope that the next time I write it will be from a liberated region. Fond kisses from your loving son.

The monument at Chevreux.

Next day, the *8e régiment* was checked with heavy losses. Among those who fell was *Sous-lieutenant* Mairet. 'Officer of magnificent courage' reads his citation. 'Led his *section* to the assault with the finest spirit and the most gallant scorn for danger; fell mortally wounded as he reached the German positions.'

The *208e régiment* attacked on the right of the *8e*, but had a reputation for being unlucky. Badly mauled during the Battle of the Somme, and again in February 1917, it had been brought back up to strength but lacked enough time to become a cohesive unit. 'Men in the rest of the division talked about this regiment discreetly,' noted an officer, 'as if discussing an invalid who had failed to make a proper recovery.' It disintegrated during the attack.

Stops 21–26
Behind the
German Front

Stop 21: Laon

Perched on an isolated hill, Laon soars majestically more than 100 metres above the surrounding countryside. Starting with the German arrival on 2 September 1914, the city endured four years of occupation. Situated just 13 km behind the Chemin des Dames, it was an important road and railway hub, and for much of the war contained the headquarters of the *7. Armee*, which held this sector of the front. During 1917–18, the city was often hit by long-range French artillery fire and bombs dropped from aircraft. The railway station and the suburbs at the foot of the hill were particular targets, but the old city centre escaped lightly compared to the devastation at Soissons or Reims. Laon was finally liberated on 13 October 1918 after being abandoned by the retreating Germans.

Many wounded soldiers died in the city's hospitals, so the Germans established several military cemeteries. You will find one of these cemeteries on the slopes below the southernmost tip of the hill (follow the signs for the *Deutscher Soldatenfriedhof 1914–18 Laon–Bousson*). Created in 1917, it was enlarged after the war, partly because the French closed other cemeteries that the Germans had established within the old city.

The citadel at the eastern end of the hill was where the Germans carried out executions. French soldiers caught while wearing civilian clothes were shot, along with inhabitants who had tried to help them. The citadel's underground passages can be visited as part of a guided tour, but you are advised to make a reservation in advance through the *Office de tourisme du pays de Laon*. In the western part of the old city, German graffiti can still be seen on the entrance gateway of the *Hôtel-Dieu*, or hospital, of the *Abbaye de Saint-Martin*.

Laon cathedral today.

Stop 22: Veslud

Veslud lay 10 km from the German front line and was in a sheltered location, tucked close behind some steep-sided heights. To the rear of the church, you will find one of the most beautiful German military cemeteries on the Western Front. It contains 1,700 fallen soldiers and is unusual in that it was not expanded after the end of the war to accommodate the remains of men transferred from elsewhere. Within the cemetery is a monument to the *50. Infanterie-Division*, the *Eingreif* unit that intervened near Berry-au-Bac on 16 April 1917 (Tour II).

Stop 23: Martigny-Courpierre
Many of the destroyed churches in this region were rebuilt after the war in the bold, innovative style known as Art Deco. You will find one of the most remarkable of them at Martigny-Courpierre, on the northern side of the Ailette valley. Dating from the early 1930s, it was made using reinforced concrete.

Stop 24: Chamouille
The calvary on the heights above Chamouille was erected in 1892. Much of the graffiti covering its base was made by German soldiers during the First World War. To reach the calvary, park in Chamouille and walk up the D967. Where the road bends to the left at the north-eastern end

Graffiti on the base of the calvary at Chamouille. This soldier has identified his unit as Reserve-Feldartillerie-Regiment Nr 14. It belonged to the VII Reservekorps, which held this sector for a year from September 1914.

of the village, take the track on the left. After 180 metres, you will come to a crossing point. Turn sharp left, and walk westwards for 500 metres to the calvary. From here, a magnificent view extends across the Ailette valley to the Chemin des Dames.

Stop 25: Colligis

The solitary gateway in the centre of Colligis is the last remnant of the walled churchyard that was destroyed in the war. A German monument stands on the hill 400 metres north-east of the village, and is visible from the D19 between Colligis and Pancy-Courtecon. (Access is difficult and you are advised against trying to reach it.) The monument was erected by the *13. Reserve-Infanterie-Division*, which as part of the *VII Reservekorps* had prevented the Allies from capturing the Chemin des Dames in September 1914. The monument was inaugurated in August 1915, two months before the division left the Aisne sector. It is dedicated not simply to the division's own dead, but also to those of its opponent, the French *18e corps*. Later in the war, the Germans made a concrete shelter underneath the monument, from where they could observe the Chemin des Dames across the Ailette valley without their presence being suspected.

Stop 26: Courtecon chapel

The chapel marks the site of Courtecon, one of the lost villages that were destroyed by the war and never rebuilt. Courtecon was wiped out by the artillery bombardments of 1917, and its territory was absorbed after the war into the neighbouring *commune* of Pancy. The chapel was built in 1932–3, and marks the location of the village church.

Stops 27–31
Aisne Valley:
Western Sector

Stop 27: Soissons

Soissons has often been besieged, for it guards the crossing point of the Aisne river on one of the great invasion routes to Paris. Following the Battle of the Marne, the French reoccupied the city on 12 September 1914 but were unable to gain the heights 3 km further north. Until the Germans withdrew to the *Siegfried-Stellung* in March 1917, Soissons remained dominated by these heights and exposed to bombardment. In 1918, the city fell to the Germans on 29 May and endured two months of occupation before being liberated on 2 August.

Start your visit inside the cathedral, where a plaque shows the damage inflicted by the bombardments. An immense gash through the

Under German bombardment: Soissons in September 1914. A view to the north-east from the Eglise Saint-Jean-des-Vignes.

German-held heights

Aisne river

Soissons: the ruins of the cathedral.

Inside Soissons cathedral. This pillar collapsed when hit by a German shell in February 1915.

nave practically cut the building in two. The repairs took almost twenty years, and traces of shell-damage remain obvious even today. From the cathedral, walk 225 metres eastwards to the British memorial facing the river. It commemorates more than 3,800 missing soldiers from the Third Battle of the Aisne and the Second Battle of the Marne in 1918.

Return to the cathedral and walk to the *place Saint-Christophe*, 300 metres to the north-west, where you will find a monument to the reconstruction of the devastated regions after the war. In the centre is depicted Guy de Lubersac, one of the leading figures in this work. The sheer scale and complexity of the task made it daunting. As the novelist Roman Dorgelès described in *Le reveil des morts* (1923), the inhabitants struggled against bureaucracy and exploitation as they tried to rebuild their lives. To give themselves more bargaining power, they formed cooperative reconstruction societies, and it was de Lubersac's initiative that resulted in the creation in 1919 of a large umbrella organization, the *Union soissonnaise des coopératives de reconstruction*.

Soissons cemetery lies 750 metres further west along the *avenue de Compiègne*. In the military plot beneath the French tricolour flag is the grave of *Cavalier* Serge Réal del Sarte of the *9e cuirassiers à pied*, who was mortally wounded at Laffaux (Tour III).

Stop 28: Sancy-les-Cheminots
By the time of the armistice, Sancy lay in ruins. A bereaved father called Paul Busquet came to search for the grave of his son, Lucien, a soldier in the *287e régiment* who had died in November 1914 in a German field hospital established in the village church. Paul found his son's grave and resolved to help the local mayor rebuild the destroyed village. Since he worked as a manager in the railways, he enlisted the help of the railway trade unions. Sancy rose again from the ruins, and in 1929 was renamed Sancy-les-Cheminots in honour of the railwaymen who had adopted it. The *mairie* – the first building to be finished – was inaugurated in 1922 and doubled as a schoolhouse. Carved above the entrance is a railway engine, and on display inside is the *commune*'s coat-of-arms, which incorporates the cross-section of a rail surmounted by a star. A garden of remembrance was opened in 1925 on the hillside at the northern edge of the village. Here you will find Lucien Busquet's tomb and memorials to other victims of the war, including two grandsons of the Italian revolutionary Giuseppe Garibaldi and the youngest son of former US President Theodore Roosevelt.

Stop 29: Fort de Condé
In the wake of France's defeat in 1871, *Général de division* Raymond Séré de Rivières created a new system of fortifications to protect it from the danger of another invasion. Fort de Condé and Fort de la Malmaison formed part of a second defensive curtain some 60–120 km behind the

Entrance to Fort de Condé.

northern frontier. With their interlocking fields of fire, these two forts dominated the valleys of the Aisne, Vesle and Ailette, and controlled the invasion corridor leading south-westwards from Belgium to Soissons and Paris.

Both forts were decommissioned before the start of the war, having been made obsolete by the discovery in the 1880s of a more powerful explosive called melinite. At the start of the Nivelle offensive, Fort de Condé lay at the south-western tip of the Vailly salient, and was the closest point on the Western Front to Paris. (The capital lies just 100 km away.) The Germans withdrew from this exposed salient on 18 April, and that evening a French detachment penetrated inside the fort and found it abandoned.

The fort had several important visitors in the autumn, since it offered views of the sector due to be attacked during the Malmaison offensive. Raymond Poincaré, the President of the French Republic, brought King Vittorio Emanuele III of Italy at the end of September, and a month later the commander of the American Expeditionary Force, General John J. Pershing, came on the actual day of the attack.

Fort de Condé fell to the Germans on 28 May 1918 when the Allies were driven off the Chemin des Dames. It survived the war more intact than Fort de la Malmaison and is now open to visitors.

Stop 30: Vailly-sur-Aisne

During the First Battle of the Aisne, Vailly was occupied by the British 3rd Division on 13 September 1914. A brigade of the French *69e division* took over this part of the line from the British on 12 October, but at the end of the month was thrown back over the river by a German attack. A monument to the three infantry regiments of this battered French brigade now stands in the *place du 306e RI* near the bridge.

At the start of the Nivelle offensive, Vailly lay within a German salient that bulged out in front of the western half of the Chemin des Dames. The French refrained from making a direct attack on the town, and instead tried to pinch out the salient from either flank. The pressure forced the Germans to fall back to the top of the plateau.

In the western outskirts of Vailly are a couple of British and French

Sergent Jacquinot's monument at Vailly.

military cemeteries. The French cemetery contains a monument to *Sergent* Félix-Germain Jacquinot of the *120e bataillon de chasseurs à pied*, who is buried a few plots away in Grave 346. He fell on 8 July 1917, when the Germans attacked the Chemin des Dames between Le Panthéon and Froidmont during the ongoing struggle for control of the observation points.

Stop 31: Vernes and Peinaud tomb

From Vailly, drive eastwards along the D925 for 2.25 km, then turn left on to the D885 (signposted for Ostel). After heading north for 1 km, the road bends round to the east. Turn left at this point, on to the minor road that leads uphill towards Folemprise farm. As you approach the edge of the wood, you will come to the joint tomb of two French airmen, *Lieutenant* Marcel Vernes and his pilot, *Sergent* Jean Peinaud. They were killed on 24 March 1917, three weeks before the Nivelle offensive, while on a reconnaissance mission to take aerial photographs. Brought down in an air battle, they crashed 2 km within German lines, and their graves were found after the French offensive overran the site. Following the war, Vernes' wealthy family erected the impressive stone tomb that you see today.

'They rise into the air like eagles': the tomb of Vernes and Peinaud.

Stop 32

Soupir

Soupir was one of the most formidable sectors assaulted by the French on 16 April 1917. From the Chemin des Dames, a great arm of the plateau extends more than 2 km to the south and then splits into three heights that dominate the Aisne valley. These three bastions – Les Grinons in the west, Mont Sapin in the centre, and the Bois des Gouttes d'Or in the east – tower up to 110 metres above the villages of Soupir and Chavonne on the valley floor. The French at the foot of the slopes were exposed to German observation, and had the marshy Aisne valley right behind them, which meant that their communication trenches were often flooded.

Soupir, 16 April 1917.

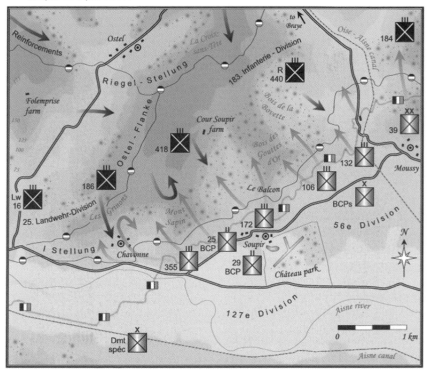

WHAT HAPPENED

Soupir lay on the eastern flank of the German salient that protruded as far as the Aisne at Vailly. The *6e corps* at Soupir formed one prong of a giant pincer move intended to collapse this salient by attacking both its flanks. Two divisions of the corps undertook the assault: the *127e division* on the left and the *56e* on the right.

The outstanding achievement on the first day of the offensive was the storming of Mont Sapin by the *25e bataillon de chasseurs à pied*. Results elsewhere were more mixed. Many French units were enfiladed by machine-guns, or checked by barbed wire hidden in the woods that covered the steep slopes. 'We were floundering in the mud, yet had to advance and follow our mates,' wrote *Capitaine* Jacques Terrasse. 'Men fell. The area was strewn with bodies.' On the western flank, a battalion of the *355e régiment* took the ruined village of Chavonne, only to be thrown out again by a German counter-thrust.

Progress was particularly disappointing in the *56e division*'s sector. The division ordered a renewed artillery bombardment so it could relaunch the attack later in the day. But *Général de division* Charles

Preparatory pounding: French shells hit the slopes of Mont Sapin, behind the houses of Soupir.

Mangin, the commander of the *6e armée*, found the delay intolerable. He believed that the troops simply lacked determination, and he emphasized the need to infiltrate between the machine-guns and bypass pockets of resistance. 'If the barbed wire is not destroyed,' he added, 'have it cut by the infantry. It is essential to gain ground.' But exhortations could not change the harsh reality of the situation, nor prevent another push that evening from ending in failure.

The French attacked again in the afternoon of 17 April. This time, they concentrated their heaviest efforts on specific locations and tried to outflank the most obstinate areas of resistance. The most significant success occurred in the Bois de la Bovette, where two battalions of the *56e division* broke into the German position and reached the crest of the plateau, thus turning the strong defences that had frustrated its attacks the previous day. On the division's eastern flank, the neighbouring *20e corps* also made important gains on the far side of the Oise–Aisne canal. That night, the increasingly beleaguered Germans began withdrawing to a fallback position on top of the Chemin des Dames. The elimination of the Vailly salient enabled the French to advance their front line by up to 5 km. Such gains, achieved despite the daunting terrain, expose the falsehood of the notion that the Nivelle offensive was a total failure.

WHAT TO SEE

Start your visit at the church in Soupir, where you will find a car park and picnic area. The church walls are still scarred from the shelling, and some of the British soldiers who fell in the First Battle of the Aisne are buried in the graveyard. Others can be found in the civilian cemetery, which you can reach if you walk 75 metres north along the *rue de Paris* and then turn right at the Commonwealth War Graves sign. Among the men buried here is Lieutenant George Brooke of the 1/Irish Guards, a distant relative of Field Marshal Sir Alan Brooke, the Chief of the Imperial General Staff in 1941–6 (they belonged to different branches of the Brooke family). The cemetery lies only part of the way up the hillside. On 16 April 1917, the Germans were 200 metres further north, holding a position so dominant that it was known as *Le Balcon*. Yet even slopes this steep could not prevent the *172e régiment* from overrunning the 'balcony' after the front-line trenches had been smashed by the preliminary bombardment.

Ruins of the Château de Soupir.

The surviving archway from the château park.

Back in the village centre, walk 150 metres south-westwards from the church to the local war memorial. A plaque fixed to the base pays tribute to the men of the *127e division*, and adds that the *237e régiment d'artillerie de campagne* was the first artillery unit to reach the conquered positions. On 19 April, after the Germans had fallen back to the Chemin des Dames, this artillery regiment managed to push one of its three *groupes* up to the top of the plateau at La Cour Soupir in order to support the infantry. The steepness of the slopes made it necessary to use up to eighteen horses to pull each vehicle.

Next to the war memorial is an iron gateway from the local *château*. Although the *château* was destroyed in the war, you can still see a solitary stone archway south-east of the church in what used to be the park, and also some rusty iron railings at the edge of the D925, which formed the southern boundary of the *château* grounds.

Four military cemeteries are clustered around Soupir: two French, one German, and one Italian. The first three lie south of the village, on either side of the D925. The German cemetery contains over 11,000 dead, over half of whom lie in a mass grave. A similar number lie in the two French cemeteries combined. (Soupir II, on the southern side of the D925, had to be created when Soupir I became full.) Only some of these men died in the immediate vicinity. The French policy after the war was to collect their own fallen, and those of the Germans, from numerous, scattered burial places into a few, large cemeteries, such as those at Soupir.

The Italian military cemetery at Soupir.

The Italian cemetery lies 1 km further west, at the point where the D88 from Soupir joins the D925. Italy entered the war on the Allied side in May 1915. Two years later, its defeat at Caporetto in October–November 1917 resulted in the despatch of eleven French and British divisions to help stabilize the situation. Most of these divisions were recalled from Italy when the Germans unleashed their offensives on the Western Front in the spring of 1918. As a gesture of solidarity, the Italian government also sent one of its own army corps, with a strength of some 50,000 men. The corps arrived in France in April 1918, and suffered heavy losses in the Second Battle of the Marne that summer. In September, it took over this sector of the Aisne valley and at the end of the month pushed a detachment across the river at Vailly to attack the Germans from the western flank. The Italians took Soupir on 1 October, and ten days later occupied the crest of the Chemin des Dames at Cerny before continuing the pursuit to the north-east. More than 9,000 men of the Italian corps died in France. Nearly 600 of them are buried at Soupir. The cemetery also contains a monument to the fallen from the women of Italy.

Memorial in the Italian cemetery.

Stops 33–38
Aisne Valley:
Eastern Sector

Stop 33: Œuilly

The French military cemetery at Œuilly lies on the hillside above the Aisne valley. From Œuilly village, head 1 km west along the D925 and turn right when you see the signpost for the cemetery. Go up the narrow, winding road, and turn sharply to the right just before the tarmacked surface gives way to stones. There is room to park at the cemetery entrance.

Behind the rows of graves is a monument to the 1st Battalion of the *163e régiment*, which belonged to the *161e division*. In August 1917, the regiment was in the Cerny sector midway along the Chemin des Dames. After capturing a German-held trench on the 10th, it repelled an initial counter-attack only to come under a sustained assault on the morning of the 13th. The Germans used flamethrowers, and dispensed with a preliminary artillery bombardment in order to ensure surprise. Six hours of fighting ended when the *163e* drove the Germans back and regained its front-line trenches. In doing so, it lost over 150 officers and men, including 21-year-old Joseph Villepelet, who is commemorated by a plaque on the monument.

Above the cemetery is a limestone cliff-face. Since the cliff faced south, away from the Germans, the French established a command post in one of its *creutes*. To reach this cavern, return to the road at the western entrance of the cemetery and walk further uphill. After 175 metres, turn right on to a track closed to vehicles by a red-and-white barrier. Some 300 metres along this track, you will pass a viewpoint over the Aisne valley on your right. Continue another 50 metres and then take the turning to the left, which leads through the bushes to the *creute*. You are not permitted to enter the *creute*, but much of it can be seen from the outside, including the pillars that were added to support

French military cemetery at Œuilly. On the right is Villepelet's monument.

La Chaouïa.

the roof. It was called La Chaouïa after a region in Morocco, and the name can still be seen carved in French and Arabic on a rock. (The initials PC stand for *poste de commandement.*)

Stop 34: Piketty gravesite

Drive north-eastwards from Beaurieux along the D892, and after 2 km the road slopes downhill and then bends sharply round to the right. At the end of the crash barrier on the lefthand side of the road is a narrow grass track leading westwards into the woods. Walk 100 metres along it and you will find a little clearing, in the middle of which is a simple stone slab lying on the ground, bearing a cross and an inscribed plaque. This is the initial grave of *Aspirant* Jean Piketty, the 19-year-old commander of a *section* of guns of the *28e régiment d'artillerie de campagne.* He fell on 15 August 1917, when his battery's fire provoked the Germans into bombarding its position in the woods. His remains have apparently been transferred to his family's tomb in Père-Lachaise cemetery at Paris.

Stop 35: Maizy

The old church was destroyed in 1940, but its ruins have been left standing at the southern end of Maizy. From the village centre, take the *rue de la vieille église* on the right of the war memorial. Follow the road for 600 metres until it bends round to the right and brings you to a T-junction. Turn right, and you will soon see the ruined church.

Commandant Bossut, who fell leading the tank attack on 16 April 1917, was initially buried in Maizy churchyard, but was reinterred after the war at his home town of Roubaix in northern France. (See Tour II.) His former burial place south-west of the church is now occupied by one of his subordinates, *Sous-lieutenant* Louis Giroud of AS2, who fell on the same day.

A low wall separates the churchyard from the adjoining civilian cemetery to the south. A plaque on the southern side of this wall commemorates three executed soldiers of the *18e régiment.* The unit had taken part in the capture of Craonne and the plateau de Californie at the beginning of May, and had then been sent to rest 24 km south of the Aisne. On the 27th, disorders broke out at Villers-sur-Fère, fuelled by alcohol and wild rumours, after the men heard that they were to return to the front. A mixture of force and persuasion eventually brought the trouble to an end. Five men were condemned to death, and the three listed on the plaque were shot at Maizy on 12 June. Another had his sentence commuted, and the fifth, a 29-year-old *caporal* called Vincent Moulia, managed to escape on the night before he was due to be executed. He ended up in Spain, and returned to France only in 1936 after the start of the Spanish Civil War.

Stop 36: Beauregard farm

Beauregard farm lies 2.5 km south-south-east of Maizy. Running past the farm is a road linking Muscourt with Fismes. At the bend next to the farm, a minor tarmacked road branches off to the west-north-west. It soon becomes a track that leads along the northern edge of the heights above the Aisne valley. If you walk along the track for just over 1 km, you will come to one of the best vantage points on the battlefield. It was from this area that the artist François Flameng witnessed the start of the offensive on 16 April 1917, and his painting is reproduced in the colour plate section of this book.

In 1917, another superb viewpoint lay 4.5 km further east, at the moulin de Roucy. Several French parliamentarians watched the attack from here on 16 April, including Georges Clémenceau, who at the time was President of the Army Commission in the Senate. You can still see the ruins of the *moulin* – an old mill – but you will find that most of the views from this point are now obscured by trees.

Stop 37: La Ville-aux-Bois

During the Third Battle of the Aisne in 1918, the 2/Devons were almost wiped out on a hill 500 metres outside La Ville-aux-Bois as the German attack swept in from the north-east. A stone cross inside the village pays tribute to the battalion, while a plaque on the wall of the *mairie* remembers 5 (Gibraltar) Field Battery of the Royal Artillery, which distinguished itself in the same action.

The design of the 2/Devons' cross failed to impress the Battle Exploit Memorials Committee, the central body created in 1919 to consider applications from units that wanted to erect permanent battlefield memorials. 'It certainly is not very beautiful,' complained the secretary in November 1920. The chairman added a sarcastic comment:

2/Devons monument at La Ville-aux-Bois, with the Croix de guerre carved on the base.

> The design certainly does not do us much credit. This raises the question as to whether we have any responsibility for designs, & are justified in plastering France with hideous monuments, such as that of the Tank Corps at Pozières, or should the French protect themselves.

The remarks were not entirely fair, since the very simplicity of the monument has its merits. Carved from Devon granite, it bears on one side of its base the *Croix de guerre*, the French decoration bestowed on the battalion. The monument has been moved here from its original location. When unveiled in 1921, it stood 1 km to the north-east at the crossroads with the D1044. Near its former site is a Commonwealth cemetery.

Stop 38: Bois des Buttes
The Bois des Buttes is an isolated hill lying in the plain between the Chemin des Dames and the Aisne. It was here that the 2/Devons made their famous stand on 27 May 1918. Until the Nivelle offensive a year earlier, the hill had been in the German front line. It was a formidable stronghold, for the Germans burrowed out a vast system of tunnels and shelters beneath it. The Bois des Buttes was captured on 16 April 1917

by the *31e régiment*, though the adjacent village of La Ville-aux-Bois held out until the morning of the 18th. A monument to the *31e régiment* is in the French military cemetery at Pontavert (Tour II).

The Bois des Buttes is now dense woodland, but was bare in 1918, for its trees had been smashed by bombardments or used by the Germans to build their tunnels. You are not permitted to enter the wooded hill, which is used partly for hunting, but you can drive along the D89 at its foot. At the western edge of the road is a monument to Guillaume Apollinaire, one of the foremost literary figures of the early 1900s. His real name was Wilhelm Apollinaris de Kostrowitzky – he was illegitimate and was descended through his mother from the minor Polish nobility. He settled in Paris, but was granted French nationality only in March 1916. As a foreigner, he had no obligation to fight for France when war broke out, yet he enlisted voluntarily in December 1914. He initially served in the artillery, but in November 1915 was promoted to *sous-lieutenant* in the *96e régiment*. On 17 March 1916, he was reading a newspaper at the Bois des Buttes when a shell-splinter pierced his helmet and wounded him in the head. 'I did not realize I had been hurt,' he later explained, 'and I was about to resume reading when suddenly my blood began gushing out.' He never fully recovered. Two years later, still weakened by the after-effects, he fell victim to the influenza epidemic and died a couple of days before the armistice, aged 38. He is buried in Père-Lachaise cemetery in Paris. The monument at the Bois des Buttes was erected in 1990, and is a tribute to Apollinaire from another writer, Yves Gibeau, who lived locally. Quoted on the stone is an extract from Apollinaire's poem *Rêverie*.

Bois des Buttes in 1917.

Stops 39–46
South of the Aisne

This final chapter highlights a handful of the most interesting points along the front between the Aisne at Berry-au-Bac and the city of Reims 19 km to the south-east. On 16 April 1917, this sector was attacked by the *5e armée*, but with limited success. The French had excellent views of this part of the German position from the heights south of the Aisne. But their attacks were complicated by the obstacle of the Aisne–Marne canal, which ran alongside the front, and by the bastions of high ground on the German flanks – Hill 108 and Mont de Sapigneul in the north, and the even more formidable height of Fort de Brimont in the south.

Stop 39: Hill 108

Hill 108 was notorious as the scene of some of the most intensive mine warfare on the Western Front. It was already notched by several quarries before 1914, and as the war progressed the two sides strove to dig

Hill 108 today.

Bois des Buttes (5.5 km)

Berry-au-Bac

Aisne river

Aisne canal

NW

View from Hill 108, around the end of the war.

deeper and deeper shafts. The hill became pockmarked with immense craters, and its much-blasted slopes were a dazzling white from the exposed limestone. At the time of writing, the hill is not open to visitors, but its northern side can be seen from the canal that runs alongside the Aisne. Its importance as an observation point is obvious.

Stop 40: Sapigneul

Sapigneul used to stand 2 km south-east of Berry-au-Bac, on the western bank of the Aisne–Marne canal. All that now remains of the village is a section of wall rebuilt using stones from the ruins. 'Here stood Sapigneul' reads the inscription on a plaque. 'In memory of the unknown soldiers who lie here, and to the glory of all those – French, British, Russian – who fought here, 1914–1918.' (Two Russian infantry brigades took part in the Nivelle offensive in April 1917. The French government had been keen to use Russian manpower on the Western Front and in the Balkans, but only a token force of 50,000 troops was actually sent.)

Stop 41: Cormicy

At the eastern entrance of Cormicy, a monument alongside the D32 remembers the men of the *69e division* who died here in September 1914. One of the division's brigade commanders, *Général de brigade*

Jean-Louis Rousseau, is buried in the civilian cemetery in the north-eastern outskirts of the village. Several other French soldiers lie in the same cemetery, and near its centre you will find the mass grave of six men of the *332e régiment*. They fell at Cormicy on 4 September 1914, and belonged to a party that had found itself cut off as the Germans swept through northern France in the weeks before the Battle of the Marne. The story of what happened is one of the minor epics of the war, and began on 31 August when a company of the *332e* under *Capitaine* Henri Klipffel was detached near Laon to escort a convoy. On 2 September, the convoy was attacked 10 km south of Laon. Klipffel's company was forced to barricade itself inside the village of Monthenaut, but fought off a German assault. It then retreated south-eastwards in the direction of Reims. Marching by night to evade the German columns, it managed to cross the Aisne by an unguarded ferry at Cuiry. On the morning of the 4th, it was attacked at Cormicy and lost sixteen men killed, wounded or missing. Klipffel left at once, changed direction to the east and on 15 September finally rejoined the French army near

Cormicy: the grave of six soldiers of the 332e régiment.

Sainte-Menéhould. Along the way, he had picked up as many as ninety-one stragglers from twenty-one different regiments.

Stop 42: Cauroy

Three commanding officers of the *5e régiment* are buried in the local civilian cemetery. They all fell in this sector within a single fortnight in September 1914, and share the same tomb. *Colonel* Ernest-Lucien Doury was the first to die, as a result of a shell-burst on the 14th. *Lieutenant-colonel* Maurice de Lardemelle assumed command on the 16th, only to fall the next day. *Lieutenant-colonel* Emile-Nicolas-Adolphe Bouteloupt took over on the morning of the 18th. Despite being wounded that

Three colonels of the 5e régiment are buried in this tomb at Cauroy.

same day, he remained in charge until killed in the night of the 25/26th. His provisional replacement, a *capitaine*, lasted barely three hours before being severely wounded.

Stop 43: Loivre

On 16 April 1917, Loivre was captured by the *41e division* (part of the *7e corps*). The division mounted a two-pronged attack to pinch out the village from either flank. On the left wing, which made the main thrust, the *23e régiment* crossed the canal and swept round behind Loivre, while the 3rd Battalion of the *133e* took the village from the north-west. One of the toughest points of German resistance was the hillock where the local war memorial now stands at the western end of the *rue du 11 novembre 1918*. One of the memorial's inscriptions remembers the *133e régiment*, which had won fame as the *régiment des lions* as a result of its feats in the Vosges in 1914–15.

From the rear of the war memorial, walk 300 metres north-eastwards along the grass track down to the local cemetery. At the roadside 40 metres beyond the cemetery is an obelisk to *Capitaine* Paul Malpas, an *adjudant-major*, or battalion executive officer, in the *170e régiment*. He was killed 2 km north-west of Loivre on the morning of 4 May 1917. Another monument stands at the D30 crossroads at the south-eastern exit of the village and commemorates the *363e régiment*, which was part of the *41e division*.

Stop 44: Berméricourt

Berméricourt fell on 16 April 1917 to the *14e division* of the *7e corps*, but was retaken by the Germans in the evening. A monument 200 metres west of the church commemorates the *35e régiment*, which seized the village. Plaques inside the church porch pay tribute to four soldiers who fell in the nearby area in April and May 1917. Outside the church is a memorial to the men of Berméricourt who died in the war, including *Sergent* Paul Gobron, who is buried just 8 km away at Berry-au-Bac (page 54).

'Remember our comrades': monument to the 35e régiment at Berméricourt.

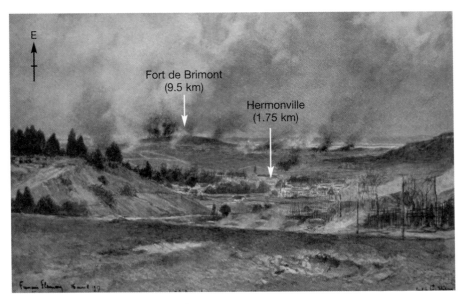

Attack by the 5e armée in the Fort de Brimont sector, 16 April 1917. A painting by François Flameng from the heights in the French rear.

Stop 45: Fort de Brimont

Fort de Brimont formed part of the girdle of fortifications protecting Reims. After the Battle of the Marne in September 1914, the French reoccupied the city but were unable to take Brimont. The fort itself was obsolete, but stood on the summit of a wooded hill that dominated the surrounding countryside. On 16 April 1917, the *7e corps* tried to capture this hill by turning its northern flank, but was checked at Berméricourt. Fort de Brimont was excluded from the renewed French onslaughts at the beginning of May, owing to concerns in political circles that attacking such a formidable position was doomed to end in a bloody failure. Brimont remained in German hands until October 1918. The actual fort is closed to the public, but the hill commands superb views, particularly towards Reims from the sports ground at the southern edge of Brimont village.

Stop 46: Reims

The Germans abandoned Reims during the night of 12/13 September 1914 after occupying it for only eight days. The city never fell again, but

remained dangerously exposed just 4 km behind the French front line.
It endured 1,051 days of bombardment – an average of over four-and-
a-half days in every week of the war – and around two in three of its
houses were destroyed. Civilian life continued despite the dangers:
around 15 per cent of the pre-war population remained at the start of
1917. But the intense German shelling at the time of the Nivelle
offensive caused a further exodus, and a complete evacuation was
ordered in March 1918. Reims was the largest French city to be
destroyed in the war, and not until the 1950s did its population figures
return to their pre-war level. The cathedral took twenty years to restore
after being shattered by the bombardments. If you have time, it is worth
making an excursion to the war museum at Fort de la Pompelle, 8 km
to the south-east along the D944.

Reims cathedral in September 1914.

FURTHER READING

Battlefield guides

The famous Michelin guides are an excellent starting point, along with their updated replacements issued in time for the centenary. Some of these titles are available only in French:

Michelin et Cie (firm). *Le Chemin des Dames*. Clermont-Ferrand, 1920.
— *Soissons before and during the war*. Clermont-Ferrand, 1919.
— *Rheims and the battles for its possession*. Clermont-Ferrand, 1919.
— *La Marne et la Champagne: les champs de bataille*. Boulogne-Billancourt, 2011.
— *Chemin des Dames, Aisne, Oise: les champs de bataille*. Boulogne-Billancourt, 2014.

English-language guidebooks tend to focus on the British participation in the First Battle of the Aisne. Jerry Murland's excellent *Aisne 1914* was published in 2013. It can be supplemented with the detailed account produced by the British War Office: *Battle of the Aisne, 13th–15th September, 1914: tour of the battlefield* (1935).

Official histories

France: Ministère de la guerre. *Les armées françaises dans la grande guerre*, 11 tomes. Paris, 1922–37. Tome 5, vols 1 and 2, and the related volumes of annexes.
Germany: Reichsarchiv. *Der Weltkrieg, 1914 bis 1918*, 15 vols. Berlin, 1925–44. Vols 11, 12 and 13.

General background

Lupfer, Timothy T. *The dynamics of doctrine: the change in German tactical doctrine during the First World War*. Fort Leavenworth, Kansas, 1981.
Stevenson, David. *1914–1918: the history of the First World War*. 2004. Reissued London, 2012.
Sumner, Ian. *They shall not pass: the French army on the Western Front, 1914–1918*. Barnsley, 2012.

Wynne, Graeme Chamley. *If Germany attacks: the battle in depth in the west*. London, 1939. Reissued Brighton, 2008, ed. Robert Foley, with the inclusion of previously deleted passages.

Second Battle of the Aisne

Buffetaut, Yves. *The 1917 spring offensives: Arras, Vimy, le Chemin des Dames*. Trans by Bernard Leprêtre. Paris, 1997.

ed. Defente, Denis. *Le Chemin des Dames, 1914–1918*. 2003. Reissued Paris, 2010.

Goes, Gustav. *Chemin des Dames*. Hamburg, 1938. (*Das Heldenlied des Weltkrieges*, vol 3).

Hellot, Frédéric Emile Amédée. *Le commandement des généraux Nivelle et Pétain, 1917*. (*Histoire de la guerre mondiale*, vol 3). Paris, 1936.

Lachaux, Gérard. *Les creutes: Chemin des Dames et soissonnais*. Cerneux, 2005.

— *Chemin des Dames: l'album souvenir du front de l'Aisne*. Paris, 2008.

The trio of French awards for heroism. From left to right (in order of precedence): the Légion d'honneur, the Médaille militaire and the Croix de guerre. Attached to the ribbon of the Croix de guerre is a bronze palm – a traditional symbol of victory, indicating that the medal has been awarded for a citation in army orders.

Légé, Daniel and Nelly. *1914–1918 en pays laonnois*. Saint-Cyr-sur-Loire, 2007.

ed. Loez, André and Nicolas Mariot. *Obéir/désobéir: les mutineries de 1917 en perspective*. Paris, 2008.

Nobécourt, René-Gustave. *Les fantassins du Chemin des Dames*. 1965. Reissued Luneray, 1983.

ed. Offenstadt, Nicolas. *Le Chemin des Dames: de l'événement à la mémoire*. 2004. Reissued Paris, 2012.

Pedroncini, Guy. *Pétain: général en chef, 1917–1918*. 1974. Reissued Paris, 1997.

Rolland, Denis. *La grève des tranchées: les mutineries de 1917*. Paris, 2005.

— *Nivelle: l'inconnu du Chemin des Dames*. Paris, 2012.

Smith, Leonard V. *Between mutiny and obedience: the case of the French Fifth Infantry Division during World War I*. 1994. Reissued Princeton, NJ, 2014.

Tour I: Marchand's division

Antier-Renaud, Chantal and Christian Le Corre. *Les soldats des colonies dans la première guerre mondiale*. Rennes, 2008.

Blankenstein, Dr Werner, et al. *Geschichte des Reserve-Infanterie-Regiments Nr 92 im Weltkriege, 1914–1918*. Osnabrück, 1934.

Charbonneau, Jean-Eugène, et al. *Les troupes coloniales pendant la guerre 1914–1918*. Paris, 1931.

Dardant, Louis.'Mémoires d'un combattant de 1914–1918, ou l'épopée du 4e zouaves' (ed. Chanaud, Robert), in ed. Labie, François and Frédérique. *Destins ordinaires dans la grande guerre*. Limoges, 2012, pp.137–247.

Delebecque, Jacques. *Vie du général Marchand*. Paris, 1936.

Deroo, Eric and Antoine Champeaux. *La force noire: gloire et infortunes d'une légende coloniale*. Paris, 2006.

Echenberg, Myron. *Colonial conscripts: the Tirailleurs Sénégalais in French West Africa, 1857–1960*. London, 1991.

France: army. *Historique du 33e régiment d'infanterie coloniale pendant la guerre 1914–1919*. Rochefort-sur-Mer, 1920.

— *Historique du 52e régiment d'infanterie coloniale: campagne 1914–1918*. Paris, nd.

— *Historique du 53e régiment d'infanterie coloniale pendant la guerre 1914–1919*. Rochefort-sur-Mer, 1920.

Germany: army. *Das 8. Lothringische Infanterie-Regiment Nr 159 im Frieden und im Weltkrieg*. Berlin, 1935.

Ingold, Capitaine. 'La division Marchand dans la 2e bataille de l'Aisne', in *Revue des troupes coloniales* (Dec 1938), no. 257, pp. 1077–1101.

von Loebell, Egon, et al. *Das 3. Garde-Regiment zu Fuß im Weltkriege*. Oldenburg, 1923. Part 2.

Mangin, Charles. *Lettres de guerre, 1914–1918*. Paris, 1950.

Michel, Marc. *Les Africains et la grande guerre: l'appel à l'Afrique, 1914–1918*. Paris, 2003.

Möller, Hanns. *Königlich Preußisches Reserve-Infanterie-Regiment Nr 78 im Weltkrieg 1914–1918*. Berlin, 1937.

Reinhard, Wilhelm. *Das 4. Garde-Regiment zu Fuß*. Oldenburg, 1924.

Tézenas du Montcel, Joseph. *L'heure H: étapes d'infanterie, 14–18*. 1960. Reissued Paris, 2007.

Thilmans, Guy and Pierre Rosière. *Les sénégalais et la grande guerre: lettres de tirailleurs et recrutement, 1912–1919*. Gorée, 2012.

Tour II: Tank assault

Basteau, Roger. 'Témoignage et réflexions sur le premier engagement des chars aux côtés de l'infanterie le 16 avril 1917', in *Le Casoar: bulletin de liaison trimestriel de la Saint-Cyrienne, Association amicale des élèves et ancien élèves de l'Ecole spéciale militaire de Saint-Cyr* (Dec 1978), no. 72, pp. 26–30.

Bavaria: Kriegsarchiv. *Das K.B. Reserve-Infanterie-Regiment Nr 10*. Munich, 1930.

Caloni, Général. 'Les ponts à la 5e armée et les sapeurs pontonniers de la compagnie 24/2 pendant la guerre', in *Revue du génie militaire* (May 1924), year 32, vol 54, 5th livraison, pp. 401–58.

Chaïla, Xavier. *C'est à Craonne, sur le plateau: journal de route 1914, 15, 16, 17, 18, 19 de Xavier Chaïla*. Carcassonne, 1997.

Chenu, Charles-Maurice. *Du képi rouge aux chars d'assaut*. Paris, 1932.

Compagnon, Jean. 'La chevauchée héroïque de Berry-au-Bac: le chef d'escadrons Bossut (16 avril 1917)', in *Revue historique des armées* (June 1984), no. 155, pp. 54–63.

Delvert, Charles. *L'erreur du 16 avril 1917*. Paris, 1920.

Demmler, Ernst, et al. *Das K.B. Reserve-Infanterie-Regiment 12*. Munich, 1934.

Deygas, Ferdinand-Joseph. *Les chars d'assaut: leur passé, leur avenir*. Paris, 1937.

Dubly, Henry-Louis.'Le Commandant Louis Bossut, héros des chars de combat', in *Septentrion: revue des marches du Nord* (Nov–Dec 1928), no. 9–10, pp. 437–42.

Dutil, Léon. *Les chars d'assault: leur création et leur rôle pendant la guerre, 1915–1918*. Nancy, 1919.

Fonsagrive, Félix. *En batterie! Verdun (1916), la Somme, l'Aisne, Verdun (1917)*. Paris, 1919.

France: army. *Historique de la compagnie 19/3 du 2e régiment du génie pendant la campagne 1914–1918*. Belfort, 1920.

Gale, Tim. *The French army's tank force and armoured warfare in the Great War: the Artillerie spéciale*. Farnham, 2013.

Galli, Henri. *L'offensive française de 1917 (avril–mai) de Soissons à Reims*. Paris, 1919.

von Guttenberg, Dr Erich Freiherr and Dr Georg Meyer-Erlach. *Das Königlich Bayerische Reserve-Feldartillerie-Regiment Nr 5*. Munich, 1938.

Hermann, Friedrich. *Das Feldartillerie-Regiment 500 im Weltkriege*. Berlin, 1927.

Lissorgues, Abbé Marcellin. *Notes d'un aumônier militaire*. Aurillac, 1921.

Möller, Hanns. *Westfalen im großen Krieg: Geschichte des Paderborner Infanterie-Regiments (7. Lothr.) Nr 158*. Berlin, 1939.

Perré, Jean-Paul. *Batailles et combats des chars français: l'année d'apprentissage, 1917*. Paris, 1937.

Perrette, Jean-François.'16 avril 1917, les chars!', in *Revue historique des armées* (March 1985), no. 158, pp. 48–60.

von Rudorff, Franz. *Das Füsilier-Regiment General Ludendorff (Niederrheinisches) Nr 39 im Weltkriege 1914–1918*. Berlin, 1925.

Schaidler, Otto. *Das K.B. Reserve-Infanterie-Regiment Nr 7*. München, 1934.

von Troilo, Hans and Dr Hans Leonhardt. *Das 5. Westfälische Infanterie-Regiment Nr 53 im Weltkrieg 1914–1919*. Oldenburg, 1924.

Tour III: Laffaux

Büttner, Ernst. *Geschichte der Brigade-Ersatz-Bataillone 32, 80 und 86 und des aus diesen hervorgegangenen preuß. Infanterie-Regiments Nr 364 während des Krieges 1914–18*. Zeulenroda, 1937.

Charbonneau, Jean-Eugène. *Etudes tactiques sur des épisodes de la grande guerre: opérations du 1er corps colonial*. Paris, 1926.

de Cossé-Brissac, Commandant. 'La Division provisoire de cuirassiers à pied au combat du moulin de Laffaux (5 et 6 mai 1917)', in *Revue de cavalerie* (Jan–Dec 1922), year 32, series 4, vol 2, pp. 299–315.

Croste, Bernard-Henri. *Pour la France ou pour des prunes: souvenirs et réflexions d'un poilu pyrénéen*. Sorèze, 1999.

Duflos, André. *A la mémoire des cuirassiers à pied*. Paris, 1919.

Fourier, Marcel and Maurice Gagneur. *Avec les chars d'assaut*. Paris 1919.

France: army. *Le 4e cuirassiers de 1914 à 1919*. Lyon, 1920.

— *Récits et faits de guerre du 9e régiment de cuirassiers, 1914–1918*. Poitiers, 1919.

— *Historique du 11e régiment de cuirassiers: campagne 1914–1918*. Paris, nd.

Lestringuez, Pierre. *Sous l'armure: les chars d'assaut français pendant la guerre*. Paris, 1919.

de Préval, Lieutenant. 'Le 4e régiment de cuirassiers à pied aux attaques de Laffaux (5 mai 1917)', in *Revue de cavalerie* (Mar–Apr 1936), year 46, pp. 131–55.

Waline, Pierre. 'Le monument des Crapouillots', in *Journal des débats politiques et littéraires* (2 Sep 1933), p. 3.

— *Les crapouillots, 1914–1918: naissance, vie et mort d'une arme*. Limoges, 1965.

Tour IV: Craonne

Delacourte, Henri. *Craonne et sa montagne: notice descriptive et historique avec plan*. np, 1908.

Durand, Pierre. *Vincent Moulia: mutins de 1914–1918*. np, 2008.

Gaudy, Georges. *Souvenirs d'un poilu du 57e régiment d'infanterie: le Chemin-des-Dames en feu, décembre 1916–décembre 1917*. Paris, 1923.

Germany: army. *Das Infanterie-Regiment von Courbière (2. Posensches) Nr 19 im Weltkriege, 1914–1919*. Görlitz, 1935.

— *Reserve-Infanterie-Regiment Nr 110 im Weltkriege 1914–1918*. Karlsruhe, 1934.

— *Das Reserve-Infanterie-Regiment Nr 111 im Weltkriege 1914 bis 1918*. Karlsruhe, 1937.

— *Das 5. Niederschlesische Infanterie-Regiment Nr 154 im Frieden und im Kriege*. Gäbersdorf, 1935.

Gibeau, Yves and Gérard Rondeau. *Chemin des Dames*. Paris, 1984.

Tour V: The Malmaison offensive

d'Arnoux, Jacques. *Paroles d'un revenant*. Paris, 1925.

Bergeder, Dr Fritz. *Das Reserve-Infanterie-Regiment Nr 202 auf den Schlachtfeldern des Weltkrieges 1914–1918*. Berlin, 1927.

Binet-Valmer. *Mémoires d'un engagé volontaire*. Paris, 1918.

von Bose, Thilo. *Das Kaiser Alexander Garde-Grenadier-Regiment Nr 1 im Weltkriege 1914–1918*. Zeulenroda, 1932.

Dardant, Louis. 'Mémoires d'un combattant de 1914–1918, ou l'épopée du 4e zouaves' (ed. Chanaud, Robert), in ed. Labie, François and Frédérique. *Destins ordinaires dans la grande guerre*. Limoges, 2012, pp. 137–247.

Fèvre, Marcel. *Voie historique de Paris aux Ardennes, de César à de Gaulle*. Paris, 1973.

France: army. *Historique du Régiment d'infanterie coloniale du Maroc, 1914–1930: 1er régiment de France*. np, nd.

— *Historique du 4e régiment de zouaves, 1914-1918*. Bizerte, nd.

— *Historique d'un régiment à fourragère rouge: le 4e régiment mixte de zouaves-tirailleurs pendant la grande guerre*. Bizerte, nd.

— *Historique du 8e régiment de marche de tirailleurs: 2e, 4e et 5e bataillons du 8e régiment de tirailleurs indigènes, campagne 1914–1918*. Bizerte, nd.

von Frantzius, Felix, et al. *Geschichte des Reserve-Infanterie-Regiments Nr 201*. Berlin, 1940.

Führer, Wilhelm. *Geschichte des Reserve Infanterie Regiments 203*, 4 parts. np, 1960–4. Part 4.

Germain, René. *Il revient immortel de la grande bataille: carnets de guerre, 1914–1919*. Triel-sur-Seine, 2007.

Germany: army. *Das 5. Niederschlesische Infanterie-Regiment Nr 154 im Frieden und im Kriege*. Gäbersdorf, 1935.

Giraud, Henri-Christian. *1914–1918: la grande guerre du général Giraud*. Monaco, 2014.

Gras, Gaston. *Malmaison: 23 octobre 1917*. Paris, 1934.

von Kaisenberg, Ernst-Moritz and Gerhard von Hirsch. *Geschichte des Grenadier-Regiments König Wilhelm I (2. Westpreußisches) Nr 7 'Königs-Grenadier-Regiment', 1797–1926*. Oldenburg, 1927.

Lunken, Walter. *Das 2. Garde-Feldartillerie-Regiment im Weltkriege*. Berlin, 1929.

Michel, Jacques. *Au service de la France: le général Guyot de Salins, 1857–1936*. Paris, 1937.

Pellegrin, Fernand-Louis-Lucien. *La vie d'une armée pendant la grande guerre*. Paris, 1921.

Prévost, Marcel. *D'un poste de commandement, PC du 21e CA: bataille de l'Ailette, 23 octobre–2 novembre 1917*. Paris, 1918.

Riebensahm, Gustav. *Infanterie-Regiment Prinz Friedrich der Niederlande (2. Westfälisches) Nr 15 im Weltkriege 1914–18*. Minden, 1931.

von Rosenberg-Lipinsky. *Das Königin Elisabeth Garde-Grenadier-Regiment Nr 3, 1914–1918*. Berlin, 1921.

von Unger, Fritz. *Das Königin Augusta Garde-Grenadier-Regiment Nr 4 im Weltkriege 1914–1919*. Berlin, 1922.

von Winterfeldt, Hans Karl. *Das Kaiser Franz-Garde-Grenadier-Regiment Nr 2, 1914–1918*. Oldenburg, 1922.

Stops

Anon. 'La construction d'une chapelle à Jeanne d'Arc à B.-M. (Aisne)', in *La grande guerre du XXe siècle* (August 1916), year 2, no. 19, pp. 150–2.

Atkinson, Christopher Thomas. *The Devonshire Regiment, 1914–1918*. Exeter, 1926.

Bonnamy, Georges. *La saignée*. Paris, 1920.

ed. Boulanger, Jean-François, et al. *Reims 14–18: de la guerre à la paix, histoire, mémoire, symboles*. Strasbourg, 2013.

Caracciolo, Mario. *Le truppe italiane in Francia: il IIo corpo d'armata, le TAIF*. Milan, 1929.

Castendyk, Hermann. *Das Kgl. Preuß. Infanterie-Regiment 'Herzog Ferdinand von Braunschweig' (8. Westfälisches Nr 57) im Weltkrieg, 1914–1918*. Oldenburg, 1936.

Napoleon's statue on the plateau de Vauclair (Stop 13).

Chagnaud, Jean-Gabriel. *Avec le 15-2: journal et lettres de guerre*. Paris, 1933.

Clout, Hugh. 'Rural reconstruction in the Aisne after the Great War', in *Rural history* (Oct 1993), vol 4, issue 2, pp. 165–85.

Cockfield, Jamie H. *With snow on their boots: the tragic odyssey of the Russian Expeditionary Force in France during World War I*. London, 1998.

Dorgelès, Roland (pseud). *Le réveil des morts*. 1923. Reissued Cuise-la-Motte, 2010.

German prisoners helping to evacuate the wounded near Soupir (Stop 32).

France: army. *Le 15-2 pendant la grande guerre de l'Alsace aux Flandres, 1914–1918.* Nancy, 1919.

— *Le régiment des lions: historique du 133e régiment d'infanterie pendant la grande guerre, 1914–1918.* Belley, 1920.

Gaucher, André and Victor-Jules-Marie Laporte. *La division du dragon, 164e, novembre 1916–janvier 1919.* Paris, 1924.

de Gaulle, Charles. *Lettres, notes et carnets, 1905–1918.* np, 1980.

Glandy, Anne André. *Maxime Real del Sarte: sa vie, son œuvre.* Paris, 1955.

ed. Jagielski, Jean-François. 'Une famille protestante dans la grande guerre: les Vernes, deux correspondances de guerre.' Published online at: www.crid1418.org.

Laby, Lucien. *Les carnets de l'aspirant Laby: médecin dans les tranchées, 28 juillet 1914–14 juillet 1919.* Paris, 2001.

de Lattre, Jean. *Ne pas subir: écrits, 1914–1952.* Paris, 1984.

Mairet, Louis. *Carnet d'un combattant, 11 février 1915–16 avril 1917.* Paris, 1919.

Malinowski, Alain. *Le Chemin des Dames: 1. La caverne du Dragon.* Louviers, 2004.

Marival, Guy. 'La Caverne du dragon', in *Graines d'histoire: la mémoire de l'Aisne* (March 1999, reissued 2000), no. 5, pp. 17–28.

Marot, Jean. *Ceux qui vivent.* Paris, 1919.

Pasquier, Henri. *Quarante-neuf mois d'esclavage: la ville de Laon sous le joug allemand.* Laon, 1922.

Pilleboue, Frédérique, et al. *Reconstructions en Picardie après 1918.* Paris, 2000.

Rogerson, Sidney. *The last of the ebb: the Battle of the Aisne, 1918.* 1937. Reissued London, 2007.

Schuhler, Abbé J. *Ceux du 1er corps: souvenirs, impressions, récits de la guerre par un aumônier militaire.* Colmar, 1931.

Taylor, Emerson Gifford. *New England in France, 1917–1919: a history of the Twenty-Sixth Division USA.* New York, 1920.

Terrasse, Jacques. *Avant l'oubli: l'histoire vécue du 355e régiment d'infanterie, grande guerre 1914–1918.* np, 1964.

Tyran, Joseph. *Laon: ville militaire.* Cambrai, 1999.

Vuillermet, Ferdinand-Antonin. *Avec les alpins.* Paris, 1918.

Wylly, Harold Carmichael. *The Loyal North Lancashire Regiment,* 2 vols. London, 1933.

Zeller, André. *Dialogues avec un lieutenant.* Paris, 1971.

USEFUL ADDRESSES AND WEBSITES

The main portal for information on visiting the Chemin des Dames is www.chemindesdames.fr. The site includes news of forthcoming events, details of local restaurants, and issues of the superb *Lettre du Chemin des Dames: bulletin d'information édité par le Conseil général de l'Aisne.*

Tourist information
Comité départemental du tourisme de l'Aisne
24–28, avenue Charles de Gaulle, 02007 Laon
Tel: 03 23 27 76 76. Website: www.evasion-aisne.com

Office de tourisme du pays de Laon
Hôtel Dieu, place du Parvis Gautier de Mortagne, 02000 Laon
Tel: 03 23 20 28 62. Website: www.tourisme-paysdelaon.com

Office de tourisme de Soissons
16, place Fernand Marquigny, 02200 Soissons
Tel: 03 23 53 17 37. Website: www.tourisme-soissons.fr

Office de tourisme de Reims
2, rue Guillaume de Machault, 51100 Reims
Tel: 03 26 77 45 00. Website: www.reims-tourisme.com

Museums, forts and caverns
Caverne du dragon (Stop 12)
Tel: 03 23 25 14 18. Website: www.caverne-du-dragon.com

Fort de Condé (Stop 29)
Tel: 03 23 54 40 00. Website: www.fortdeconde.com

Fort de la Malmaison (Tour V)
Visits organized through the Caverne du dragon.

The hill on the horizon is the Bois des Buttes, where the 2/Devons made their stand on 27 May 1918 (Stop 38).

Musée du Fort de la Pompelle (Stop 46)
Tel: 03 26 49 11 85. Website: www.reims.fr

Several lesser-known caverns in the region contain spectacular artwork and graffiti made by soldiers during the war. Some can be visited by prior arrangement, but may require more agility than the Caverne du dragon:

Carrière de Froidmont (Stop 7).
Association Chemin des Dames. Email: gilles.chauwin@sfr.fr

Carrières de Confrécourt (11.5 km west-north-west of Soissons).
Website: www.soissonnais14-18.net

Locating fallen soldiers

French: www.memoiresdeshommes.sga.defense.gouv.fr and
www.memorial-genweb.org
German: www.volksbund.de
Commonwealth: www.cwgc.org

War diaries of French units

The war diaries, or *journaux des marches et opérations,* can be found at: www.memoiresdeshommes.sga.defense.gouv.fr.

Other relevant websites

www.archives.aisne.fr (Archives of the *département* of the Aisne)

www.battlefields14-18.com or www.aisne14-18.com (*Aisne 14–18: le centenaire*)

www.centenaire.org (*Mission du centenaire de la première guerre mondiale*)

www.crid1418.org (*Collectif de recherche international et de débat sur la guerre de 1914–1918*)

www.greatwar1418.eu (100 Great War 14–18)

Note

The details given above are valid as of October 2014.

Hurtebise farm: the 1814–1914 monument (Tour I).

INDEX

Entries are filed word-by-word. **Bold** locators refer to colour plate numbers. *Italic* locators refer to page numbers of other illustrations.